LAND OF MYSTERY, TRAGEDY AND COURAGE

pakistan

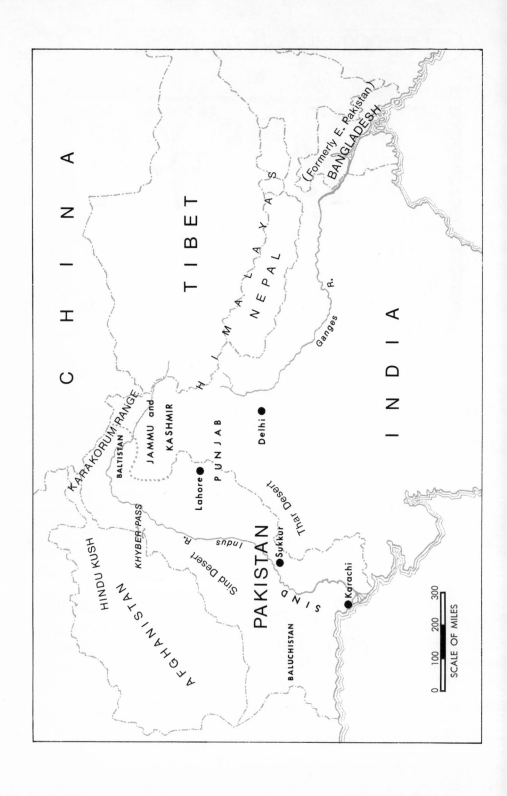

LAND OF MYSTERY, TRAGEDY AND COURAGE

Pakistan

I.G. EDMONDS

Photographs by the author

HOLT, RINEHART AND WINSTON

New York

Library of Congress Cataloging in Publication Data

Edmonds, I.   G
 Pakistan; land of mystery, tragedy, and courage.

 Bibliography: p. 165
  1. Pakistan—History—Juvenile literature.
I. Title.
DS384.E33 954.9 74-14974
ISBN 0-03-013696-2

To Annette, of course

LAND OF MYSTERY, TRAGEDY AND COURAGE

pakistan

CONTENTS

1

In the Valley of the Indus

Some 150 million years ago, in the days of the dinosaurs, there was a vast inland sea north of present-day India. Stresses and strains inside the cooling earth set up tremendous pressures that thrust this region upward to create the Tibetan plateau. The sea disappeared, draining off into a new river. This river, which became today's Indus, flowed northwest and then turned south to flow into the sea. These changes did not come in one sudden cataclysmic rupture of the earth's crust, but were spread over millions of years. Finally, about 30 million years ago, the northern mass of Asia began to slip south. It jammed against the unyielding Deccan block of South India. Caught between these two mighty forces, the earth's crust cracked, buckled, and folded over itself to thrust up into the Himalaya Mountains.

The Indus River was one of the few natural features of the land to survive this drastic remolding of the earth. The river was able to adjust to the upheaval because the uplift of the Himalayas was slow, geologically speaking. Thus the river was able to cut itself a deeper channel as the mountains climbed around it. Today, in some places, the river winds through solid rock gorges where cliffs tower 15,000 feet high on either side.

The Indus river finally solidified its course. It ran northwest out of the Tibetan Highlands, paralleling the Himalaya Range, and then curved around the western end of the Himalayas, passing within 60 miles of famous K-2 mountain in the Karakorum Range. From there it flowed through Baltistan and Kashmir before plunging into a deep rift between the mountains of Afghanistan on the west and the hills of India on the east. This great depression was then at least 6,000 feet deep, and some geologists think it may have been as much as 15,000 feet deep. It may have sunk as a result of the uplift of the great mountain ranges to the northeast. In any event, it became a vast gulf opening on the present-day Arabian Sea.

This was the time when the Indus, fighting to survive the uplift of the earth, was grinding away mountains to create its path to the sea. This grinding, cutting, and erosion moved an enormous amount of silt down the river into the great gulf. The Kabul River in Afghanistan, and the Jhelum, Chenab, Ravi and Sutlej—Himalayan tributaries of the Indus—added their own massive erosion to the silt pouring into the gulf. In time they entirely filled the gulf with alluvium to create the present land of Pakistan between the mountains of Afghanistan and the Thar Desert of India.

It seems incredible that one river and six tributaries could fill a depression nearly 1,000 miles long, 400 miles wide, and between one and two miles deep. Yet measurements made in modern times at Sukkar, about 400 miles from the Indus Delta, show the enormous power of the river. At this point, the Indus carries nearly ten million cubic feet of silt. M. B. Pithawalla, an Indian geographer, estimated that in the twenty-nine year period between 1902

*Women today carry water from the Indus just as their ancestors
have done for more than 5,000 years.*

and 1930 the Indus deposited enough silt between Sukkar and Kotri—a distance of about 200 miles—to cover 1,300 square miles of land one foot deep. The entire Indus River system, according to the Indus River Commission, moves six billion cubic feet of silt during the three months of flood flows each summer.

Originally, the valley of the Indus was a jungle, populated by wild animals and a very primitive people. In time, the changing climate destroyed the jungles and turned Pakistan into the arid land it is today. Then, prehistoric creatures gave way to a mysterious race about whom little is known. They were followed by the so-called Aryans from Persia and later by a steady succession of conquerors who used Pakistan as the gateway for attacks on India. For centuries some of the greatest names in Asian history stormed and fought in North Pakistan: Cyrus the Great, Darius the Persian, Alexander the Great, Genghis Khan, Tamerlane the Earthshaker, Babur the Tiger, Shah Jahan who built the Taj Mahal, and on down to the British field marshal, Sir Henry Hardinge, who became Governor General of India in 1844.

About 650 A.D., the Moslem religion was introduced into the land that is now Pakistan, beginning the bloody struggle between Hindus and Moslems. First one and then the other religion dominated the country, and although some rulers were more tolerant than others, the followers of the two religions could never dwell together in peace. Indeed, hatred and fear had become so great that when Great Britain agreed to give India independence in 1947, the country had to be partitioned along religious lines.

This partition, which created the nation of Pakistan, gave the Moslem minority a country where they could live under the laws of Islam, free of Hindu domination. The new nation was divided into two sections: West Pakistan included the Indus River region; East Pakistan, 1,000 miles away, on the other side of India, embraced the eastern section of the former Indian province of Bengal. At the time, this appeared to be a Solomon-like solution to the problem of religious intolerance. But instead of settling the trouble between Moslems and Hindus, partition created new

problems that resulted in four wars, inhuman cruelties and op-
pressions, and the threat of more trouble in the future.,

The climax came in 1971 when East Pakistan, supported by
India, broke away from Pakistan in a bloody civil war to become
the independent nation of Bangladesh. The nation of Pakistan
was reduced to the land drained by the Indus River and the
northern section of the province of Kashmir. This is the situation
of Pakistan today. It is a country with a tremendous history, but
one caught in the center of forces that threaten its existence.

The name "Pakistan" is an artificial word, created in 1931 by a
Moslem student in England. This young man, Rahmat Ali, was an
ardent believer in Moslem independence. In setting down a list of
countries and states he believed should be included in a Moslem
Indian nation, Rahmat Ali was struck by the fact that the first
letters of the names could be combined to form a word that
meant Land of the Pure in both Persian and Urdu, the Indo-
European language most commonly spoken in the Indus region.
The states were:

> Punjab
> Afghan
> Kashmir
> Sind
> Baluchistan.

Taking the initials of the first four, adding a gratituous "i" and
the "tan" from Baluchistan, Rahmat Ali formed the word Pakistan. The name was first used publicly in 1932 in a pamphlet
entitled: *Now or Never.* It called openly for a separation of
Hindu and Moslem India.

Pakistan today is divided into six geographic areas, with the
Northern Highlands in the north part of the divided state of
Jammu and Kashmir. The double name, Jammu and Kashmir, is
the official designation of the state commonly called Kashmir.
The southern sector is occupied by India, although claimed by
Pakistan. The Northern Highlands and Red China's Sinkiang

Farm homes in the fertile Punjab are substantially built of sun-dried and burned bricks, surrounded by protective walls.

Ninety per cent of Pakistan's people live by herding and farming.

Province share a common border in the region between the Hindu Kush and Karakorum mountain ranges. Few people live in this rugged territory because of the harsh climate.

The second geographical division is the Western Highlands that front on northeast Afghanistan. This is also rugged country, but not as harsh to man as the Northern Highlands. This section is the "Hill Country" of Rudyard Kipling and the fierce Pathans who fought the British in the Khyber Pass area, during the years when Great Britain occupied India.

East of the Western Highlands is historic Punjab—the Land of the Five Rivers. Pakistan Punjab includes only about half of the Punjab province of British days. The state was sliced in half when Pakistan separated from India in 1947. Fortunately for Pakistan, its section of Punjab includes the fertile alluvial valleys between the rivers, and it is the nation's most important source of agricultural wealth.

South of Punjab is the Thar Desert, the largest part of which is in India. Then, between the desert and the Arabian Sea, is the Rann of Kutch. Rann means salt marsh, and this land is nothing but Indus River silt that has not yet conquered the seas as the rest of the Indus Delta has done. The Rann of Kutch is desolate and inhospitable.

The central sector below Punjab is the Indus Valley, where the people live by irrigating the desert with the waters of their great river. This region is called Sind. The Aryan word Sind means "river," and it is the root from which the words Indus, Hindu, and India derive. Even such remote names as West Indies, East Indies, and American Indian trace their ancestry back to the word Sind.

East of Sind, the land of Pakistan rises up to the harsh plateau of Baluchistan. The people are mostly herders and shepherds, although there is some farming in the valleys.

Until 1971 Pakistan was the fifth largest in population of the earth's nations. The population dropped from 130 million to about 55 million when East Pakistan became the independent

Rawalpindi in the Punjab is one of the few cities in Pakistan. Here pushcart merchants do more business in the streets than in the stores.

nation of Bangladesh in December, 1971. Ninety per cent of the people are farmers and herdsmen. There are hundreds of villages strung along the Indus and cradled in the hills, but few cities of any size. The major urban areas are Karachi on the Arabian Sea, Quetta in Baluchistan, Rawalpindi near the site of the ancient caravan city of Taxila, Hydrabad on the Indus, Lahore, the ancient Mogul city in Punjab, Peshawar, the historic guardian of the fabled Khyber Pass, and Islamabad, the nation's capital.

The people are called Pakistanis by their government, but there is no actual Pakistani people as a distinct race or culture. The Pakistanis are a confederation of widely varying types who share no common ethnic, linguistic, or cultural background except the Moslem religion. Urdu—an Indo-European tongue akin to Persian—was once the official language, although spoken by only three million people. The present government has made Sindhi, spoken by five million Pakistanis, the new official language. Punjabi, most widely spoken, is the language of 23 million people. Altogether, there are 32 different tongues spoken in Pakistan, and these are further broken down into local dialects.

Despite the many languages, there are only four major ethnic groups in Pakistan. The dominant group in the Hill Country is the Pathan, the fierce warrior tribes. They are thought to be of Afghanistan origin, but some claim descent from the Greeks after Alexander the Great's conquest in 327 B.C. Other Pathan tribes claim their common ancestors was a man named Kais, a contemporary of the Prophet Mohammed. Kais, it is said, traced his own origin to King David of Jerusalem.

Also in the northern Hill Country is a tribe called the Kafirs—a word that means "unbelievers." Tall, light-haired, and blue-eyed, they are believed to be descendents of the Aryans from Iran who invaded the Indus Valley about 1500 B.C. The Kafirs nominally accept Islam in order to get along with their Moslem neighbors, but mostly they cling to their ancient pagan rites.

The Baluchis and the Brahuis dominate Baluchistan. The Baluchis are nomadic herdsmen who drive their cattle from one meager grazing ground to another. There are nine tribes of Baluchis, all claiming a common ancestry. However, they do not band together beyond membership in an individual tribe. They are understandably haughty and warlike, for they must protect their flocks and herds from invaders. The second major group in Baluchistan, the Brahuis, are also nomads. In the spring and summer, they farm valleys where they can find water. In the winter, they migrate south into Sind where they sell their cattle, sheep, and goats, and hire out as seasonal workers. In the spring, the Brahuis move back to their valleys in the high plateau region to begin their annual life cycle again.

In the Punjab area, there are no sharply defined groups such as one finds in Baluchistan and the Northwest Territory. The people resemble the Indo-Aryans of North India. The Punjabi language also comes from the same Indo-European base as Hindi. Unlike the rest of Pakistan, the Punjab does have a caste system, but it is not as strict as the separation of classes in Hindu-controlled areas. It is based upon occupation, rather than based on birth as it is in India. The majority of the Punjabis are farmers. They live in mud-brick and mud-stucco houses in small villages, spread through the agricultural valleys between the five rivers. Lahore, the provincial capital, is an historic city and the cultural center of the nation.

Sind, which encompasses the lower Indus Valley all the way to the Arabian Sea, is also inhabited by ethnically mixed people. They, too, speak an Indo-European language, but one distinct from Punjabi. The people cluster around the Indus and its tributaries and irrigation canals. Beyond the irrigated area, there is nothing but the bleak Sind Desert where temperatures reach 130 degrees F in the summer. Adding to the unpleasantness, suffocating sandstorms sweep across the land with devastating regularity. The major Sind city, Karachi, is also the nation's largest, with a population of 1.5 million. It is also the only port in Pakistan capable of receiving ocean-going ships. All imports and exports, transported by water, must pass through Karachi, a factor that has contributed much to the city's growth.

Beyond Karachi, Sind is the most primitive and economically backward province in Pakistan, but it was not always this way. Ruins of great seaports have been found along the now desolate Sind coastline. Crumbling tombs outside of Karachi hint at the glory of great kings who ruled the desert kingdoms a thousand years ago. Strangest of all are the ruins of a forgotten city, 200 miles north of Karachi. Here excavators found remnants of a totally unknown civilization that appears to be as old as Ur of the Chaldees, the biblical home of the patriarch Abraham. This strange ruin, called Mohenjo-Daro (the Mound of the Dead), is one of the most puzzling archeological mysteries in the world.

CHAPTER

2

Cities of Mystery

Archeologists dig in the rubble of the past to explain the secrets of forgotten times and people. In Troy, Nineveh, Babylon, and other lost civilizations, archeology has explained many of their secrets. But in Pakistan most of what archeologists have uncovered has added new mysteries to history. For example, what really happened in the Valley of the Indus when man was first growing out of savagery?

We know that there were men in Pakistan at the end of the last ice age. No bones have been found to show what kind of men they were, but their presence is proven by the crudely sharpened stones they left behind. In still later geological stratas, searchers found shards of characteristic pottery. This meager evidence convinced researchers that Pakistan and Kashmir were populated by

an extremely primitive people until about 1500 B.C., when the
Aryans from Iran invaded the Indus Valley through the Khyber
Pass. The story of this invasion is vaguely told in the *Rig Veda*, a
collection of sacred Hindu verses that has been called the oldest
document among living religions. The *Rig Veda* contains many
stirring tales of gods and heroes battling barbarian hordes. The
verses were written about 500 years after the Aryan invasion, and
the general theme seemed to bear out what investigators believed
had happened in North Pakistan. The more advanced Aryans,
under the leadership of a king identified with the war god Indra,
invaded Pakistan. After years of hard fighting, they succeeded in
pushing out the more primitive natives who had not advanced
beyond a stone-age culture.

Here the matter stood until 1920 when surprised diggers uncovered the lost city of Mohenjo-Daro on the west bank of the
Indus River, about 200 miles north of Karachi. The discovery was
startling, for this proved to be a true city. It was three miles in
circumference and had streets laid out in mathematical rectan-
gles. The ruins were in layers like the seven successive cities of
Troy. The top level, believed to date to 1500 B.C., was poorly
constructed and gave evidence of having been a slum area. But
deeper levels of excavation disclosed well-constructed buildings
of burned brick. This level had a remarkable drainage system
with second-floor toilets flushing through chutes to underground
sewage systems. There were also great public buildings and a
large public bath such as those later encountered in Greece and
Rome. Moreover, there were indications of a well-defined art and
religion.

The best level of Mohenjo-Daro has been dated as a thousand
years older than the poorly constructed top level. This makes the
city contemporary with Akkad, a Sumerian kingdom believed to
have been in the region that later became Babylon. This would be
about 2300 B.C., long before the rise of the Greek civilization.
Discoveries of beads and seals disclosed that there had been a
lively sea trade between Mohenjo-Daro and Akkad. The dis-

A new city was built atop the ruins of an earlier Mohenjo-Daro. This excavated wall shows the careful construction of the older brick work and the shoddy work of the later city.

covery of this lost city led to others: Harappa in North Pakistan, Chandhu-Daro, south of Mohenjo-Daro, and others showed that there had been a great nation strung along the Indus. This civilization, previously undreamed of, had lived and died at a time when archeologists were certain that only primitive tribes sparsely populated prehistoric Pakistan. These lost cities were not tightly grouped. Rather, they stretched over a thousand miles— proof that they had belonged to a large nation.

Who were the people who built these cities? Most ancient civilizations show the influences of older cultures, but the Indus civilization does not. The culture of the ancient Indus Valley bears scant resemblance to that of the people of the Tigris-Euphrates Valley, in Mesopotamia, or to the culture of southern India.

This difference even extends to the writing. The Akkadian cuneiform writing and the Egyptian hieroglyphics have been deciphered, but no one has yet succeeded in reading the Indus script of Mohenjo-Daro. No extensive clay tablets or wall inscriptions, such as those found in Mesopotamia and Egypt, have been located in Mohenjo-Daro. Examples of Indus writing, almost exclusively found on seals, apparently were used by their owners as a means of "signing" their names. The writing was usually carved above a realistic depiction of some animal. Much of the carving was intaglio—that is, sunk into the seal so that pressure on wet clay produced a final raised image. There was no particular pattern to the lettering. Some of it suggests pictographs, but on other seals the writing was made up of perpendicular lines of considerable thickness. Some of these lines appear straight and grouped tightly together; others are wavy, and still others are in the form of narrow v-lines.

Today, the area surrounding Mohenjo-Daro is barren, but 4,000 years ago it was nearly a jungle with many marshes. Crocodiles were common and wild animals, apparently including rhinoceros and elephant, were plentiful. There were thick stands of timber on the low hills.

The column of bricks that appears to be a chimney is actually a well. As rubble covered succeeding layers of past cities, new builders extended the walls of the well to match the new top level. The ground reached the top of the bricks when excavation started to uncover the lower walls.

In its golden age, the city itself had a very large and affluent middle class. There were a surprisingly large number of shops. These better-class residents and stores were stretched along the banks of the Indus. Back of the city there was an artificial hill on which public buildings were constructed. One was an enormous granary where grain was stored as a hedge against famine in poor years. Another building was a citadel that housed military troops. Beyond the citadel was a remarkable public bath that would not have been out of place in Rome, 2,000 years later.

The city's golden age seems to have coincided with that of Akkad in the time of Sargon I—about 2300 B.C. However, the Indus civilization goes back much farther than this era. Continued digging in Mohenjo-Daro indicates that there are levels far below this age. Unfortunately, these earlier ruins lie below the water table. Excavations are continually flooded with water, thus halting the work. The levels of ruins above the Sargonian period indicate that at least twice the city had been covered by devastating floods. Each time the city was rebuilt upon the rubble of previous destruction, the construction work became poorer.

The fact that the original levels of construction lie below the water table may indicate that the land has subsided since the first city was built at Mohenjo-Daro. Geological evidence shows that there has been considerable change. The course of the Indus River is much different today than it was in prehistoric times, and the coastline is now 35 miles deeper into the Arabian Sea. Another theory is that the shift of the Indus caused a rising of the water table, the level at which water is found when wells are dug. Not enough work has been done, however, to prove what actually did happen.

There is also no evidence to show what kind of people lived in Mohenjo-Daro. There are two busts in the Mohenjo-Daro museum, but since they may be either kings or priests, they are possibly atypical. One shows a grim-faced, bearded man with a low forehead and slitted, but not Oriental eyes. He has a thick nose and heavy lips downturned into a frown. His hair is combed back and is cropped in a rough bob just below the level of his ear lobes. His hair is held in place by bands which encircle his head. He is dressed in a tunic that completely covers his left shoulder and arm, but leaves the right shoulder and arm bare. The robe is decorated with numerous raised designs, suggesting three-petal flowers.

The second stone head has the same trimmed beard and shaven upper lip, but the hair is waved. The eyes are fully open and the lips are thin.

Artistically the best object found in the ruins is a small—about four inches high—bronze figurine of a naked dancing girl with somewhat Negroid features. Bronze was apparently rare in Mohenjo-Daro for this is the only bronze statue found. Since dancing girls were bought and sold, this little bronze girl is not necessarily typical of the city's women. Many terra-cotta figures were also found. Some were grotesque and may have been votive figures used in religious rites. Others were humorously depicted and may have been toys.

No bones of people were discovered in the upper levels. This indicates that the dead were burned. Some skeletons were found in the top level, dated about 1500 B.C., and these indicate that the city was destroyed by invaders. According to Archeologist Mortimer Wheeler, fourteen skeletons were found "in attitudes suggesting simultaneous and violent deaths. Two skulls showed cuts by swords."

Many skeletons give evidence of having been hastily crammed into ditches and covered up. Others appear to have been left to rot in deserted streets. In this hot climate the dead would not have been left like this, unless the city had been hastily abandoned. The inference to be drawn is that the city was under attack and the defenders buried the dead as long as they could. When the enemy broke through the defenses and swept through the city, the remaining inhabitants were probably slaughtered. The invaders evidently made no attempt to establish any residence in the sacked city, but loaded their booty and moved on.

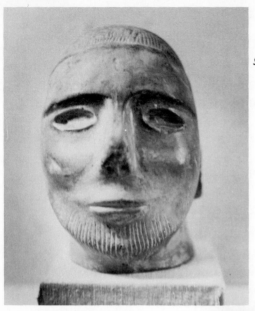

Priest, king, god, devil or hero? No one knows who or what this stone head found in Mohenjo-Daro represents.

A dancing girl, the best object found in the ruins of Mohenjo-Daro.

Archeologists believe that the destroyers of Mohenjo-Daro were the Aryans who came into the Indus Valley from the highlands of what is now Iran about 1500 B.C. Their theory is based upon the estimated time of the fall of Mohenjo-Daro and obscure references in the *Rig Veda* which tell how Indra, the Aryan war god, destroyed his enemies. These invaders were called Aryans in histories written prior to World War II. Then Nazi Germany's adoption of "Aryan" to mean all Caucasians of non-Jewish blood brought the word into disrepute. Originally, Aryan was never meant to define a race. The word means "lord or master" in Sanskrit. Today's historians usually use the term "Indo-European" in place of Aryan. But whatever we call them, they were the fathers of the Hindu religion and language in present day India.

Although clear proof is lacking, the supposition is that these invaders from Iran destroyed the entire Indus civilization from Harappa in the north to Mohenjo-Daro in the south. They then invaded India. According to this theory, the people of Mohenjo-Daro were of Dravidian stock, a dark-skinned people akin to the ancestors of the present inhabitants of South India. The light-skinned Aryans considered themselves superior to the dark-skinned natives they supplanted. This is believed to be the origin of the caste system that has plagued India ever since. The Sanskrit word for color and caste is the same.

In the years that followed the destruction of the Indus civilization, new towns—all poorly built—grew up on the sites of many of the razed cities. The industry and trade of the Indus period was gone, leaving only farmers to struggle with an environment that was growing steadily hostile. The jungles disappeared. The forests around Mohenjo-Daro had long since been destroyed to feed the great brick kilns that supplied building material for more than a thousand years. Some observers believe that this destruction of the forests was what changed the climate, turning the region into the barren land that it is today.

A thousand years passed after the fall of the Indus civilization. Northern India was developing powerful principalities under the

Hindus. The Indus Valley was divided into its own small states, some independent, some owing allegiance to ruling Hindu princes. Historically, Pakistan was stagnant. The natives dug irrigation ditches from the Indus and its tributaries, as changing climatic conditions lessened the annual rainfall. Sheep grazed on the increasingly barren hills. As the wealth and power of North India grew, the land that would someday become Pakistan developed towns to serve trade caravans that moved out of Persia and Afghanistan into India.

In the sixth century B.C., Cyrus the Great, who established the Persian empire, crossed the Khyber Pass and occupied the region around Peshawar. Later Cyrus' successor, Darius I, extended the Persian Empire to the Indus River. As Persian trade prospered in the princely states of India, caravan towns in Pakistan increased in importance. Then, after Persia collapsed, North Pakistan reverted to independent princely states until 327 B.C., when Alexander the Great invaded the subcontinent.

Alexander was then at the height of his glory. From a base in his father's kingdom of Macedonia, Alexander had conquered all of Greece, Egypt, and Babylon. Following the fall of Babylon, Alexander maneuvered for almost a year in Turkestan and Afghanistan, before invading Pakistan in the early summer of 327 B.C. His combined Greek and Macedonian troops almost mutinied, for they had been fighting for eight years. They wanted to return home to enjoy their booty, but Alexander convinced them that they could not return in honor until they reached the Indus River. The Indus had been designated as the limit of the old Persian Empire. If they gave up before they reached the Indus, they would have to acknowledge that the Persians were greater conquerors than themselves.

The grumbling ceased and Alexander split his forces. Half came into Pakistan through the fabled Khyber Pass. When Alexander led the rest through the Kabul River Valley, north of the Khyber, fierce hillmen contested their advance. Years later, Macedonian veterans of the campaign told Arrian, the Greek historian, that their hardest fighting had been in Pakistan. They did not reach the Indus until the spring of 326 B.C. Alexander halted there for thirty days to rest his troops. Then he had them construct a bridge by lashing boats together, and they crossed the great river for an attack on Taxila, near the present city of Rawalpindi.

Here Alexander was met by Prince Ambhi of Taxila, who proposed that Alexander be recognized as his overlord in exchange for providing aid in a war against Prince Porus of the adjoining Paurava—an able ruler and a renowned warrior. The Macedonian invader readily agreed, and the combined Taxilian and Greek armies made a hard-forced march through rain and mud to the Hydaspes River, an eastern tributary of the Indus. Here in the Punjab Alexander fought one of the great battles of his life.

In the battle with Alexander, Porus had every advantage. After all, he was fighting on his home ground. Moreover, there was a river between him and his enemy. In addition, he had 35,000 infantry, 300 war chariots and—most formidable of all—200 war elephants. Alexander's forces totaled only 6,000 infantry and 4,000 cavalry.

But the Macedonian did not fear the three-to-one superiority of his enemy. His only worry was the war elephants, for the Indian soldiers on the elephants had a considerable advantage over the Greeks on the ground. Worse yet, Alexander's cavalry horses, unaccustomed to elephants, panicked at the sight of the huge beasts.

Alexander and Porus drew up their opposing forces, across the river from each other, just below the present town of Jihlam in late June of 326 B.C. For several days, Alexander maneuvered along the west bank of the river, as if seeking a place to cross. Finally, Alexander made what appeared to be a permanent camp, giving the appearance that he had decided to wait for an end to the rainy season. Porus promptly camped across the river opposite him.

This suited Alexander's plan. Twenty miles north of the camp site Alexander's scouts had found a shallow place where the river was fordable. Between this ford and Porus' camp was a sandy area, known as the Plain of Karri—an ideal spot for military maneuvering in wet weather.

Alexander and the bulk of his troops marched rapidly to the ford 20 miles upstream. Porus' spies informed him of Alexander's move, but he was handicapped by the terrain. He had to march around the outside of the river's bend, while Alexander had a straight and unopposed course. In the battles that followed, the Pauravian infantry would advance, with the elephants spread out 100 feet from each other in several lines. When opposition from the Macedonians became too heavy, the infantry would fall back between the elephants for protection. The Greek historian Diodorus said the Indian army looked like a city wall: "The elephants resembled city towers and the soldiers between them resembling the walls between the towers."

In the preliminary skirmishes, before the final battle, Alexander had given particular attention to the elephants. The huge beasts had tough hides. The spears and arrows of the Macedonians could hurt and infuriate the elephants, but they could not stop them. Alexander, realizing this, concentrated his archers upon the *mahouts*, the elephant drivers. Although exposed, the mahouts were difficult to hit as they crouched low over the elephants' heads. However, once a driver was killed, the elephants became unmanageable.

The historian Arrian, who based his account of the battle upon interviews with veterans, gave this version of the final phase of the fighting: "Many of the elephant drivers had been shot down, and of the elephants themselves some had been wounded. Others from exhaustion and the loss of their mahouts no longer kept to their own side, but attacked friend and foe quite indiscriminately, pushed them, trampled them down, and killed them in all manner of ways. But the Macedonians, who had a wide and open field, and could therefore operate as they thought best, gave way when the elephants charged, and when they retreated followed at their heels and plied them with darts; whereas the Indians, who were

in the midst of the animals, suffered from the effects of the animals' rage.

"When the elephants became quite exhausted and no longer
attacked with vigor, they fell back like ships backing water and
kept trumpeting as they retreated with their faces to the enemy.
Then Alexander surrounded the enemy's line with his cavalry and
signaled that the infantry, with shields locked together so as to
give the utmost compactness to their ranks, should advance in
phalanx. . . . Upon this all the enemy turned to flight wherever a
gap should appear in the cordon of Alexander's cavalry."

Porus, riding the most majestic elephant of the corps, fought to
the end. He finally collapsed from weakness caused by loss of
blood. He was dragged before his conqueror as soon as he revived. "What shall I do with you?" Alexander asked. Porus drew
himself up to his full height and said, "Treat me as a king!" Alexander, who admired a brave enemy as much as a brave soldier in
his own ranks, was so captivated by Porus' answer that he offered
the defeated king a place in his ranks. Porus accepted. Alexander
brought about a truce between Porus and Ambhi of Taxila and
confirmed both as rulers of their states and vassals to himself.

In the course of the conquest of northern Pakistan, Alexander
had heard for the first time of the rich kingdoms of India. He was
eager to take his war of conquest into the Ganges region of India,
but at the Beas River—the most eastern of the tributaries of the
Indus—his war-weary army, which had followed him for eight
years, finally mutinied. They longed to see their homeland once
again.

Alexander was furious. Although he appeared to bow to the
inevitable, he was not yet ready to leave Pakistan. Alexander told
his men they would descend the Indus River and go home along
the coast. But his real motive was to add southern Pakistan—then
called Sind—to his kingdom. Also he knew that Darius I, when he
invaded the Indus Valley, had sent an exploration party down the
Indus. This party then took boats and followed the coast to redis-
cover the sea lane followed by traders who sailed between Ur of

the Chaldees and Mohenjo-Daro more than 2,000 years earlier.

Alexander was determined to do everything that Darius had done to prove himself the equal of the great Persian king. He first pulled back into Punjab and founded a town at the site of his victory over Porus. He then had a thousand boats built and began to descend the Indus to the Arabian Sea. It was not an easy trip. Some tribes capitulated without battle, but most of them put up a ferocious fight. About 80 miles above the present city of Multan they encountered the Malavas (also known as the Malloi) who took refuge in a walled city. In the ensuing battle, Alexander received a near-fatal wound in the chest. In contrast to Alexander's policy of trying to win over those he conquered, his furious soldiers put every man, woman, and child in the city to the sword. After this frightful slaughter, there was little opposition as the Macedonians continued on to the shore of the Arabian Sea.

Alexander arrived in Babylon in May, 324, and died the following year. Immediately his generals began a power struggle that ended with a division of the Alexandrian Empire. Seleucos Nikator got the portion that included Pakistan, but it did him little good. As soon as word reached Pakistan that Alexander was dead, the conquered provinces were in revolt.

The Hindu Years

By the time of Alexander the Great, the Aryans, who swept into India through Pakistan in 1500 B.C., had control of all of northern India. However, no great empire was formed because the conquered land was broken up into hundreds of small princely states that were continually destroying themselves in the continuous wars that characterized the age.

During these years, the original Vedic pagan beliefs of the Aryan invaders were solidifying into what would become modern Hinduism. The warrior Indra was the chief god of the Aryans. In time Indra faded into the background to survive as the god of thunder and lightning. His place was taken by a trinity: Brahma the Creator, Vishnu the Preserver, and Shiva the Destroyer. In addition, there were hundreds of other gods, but many were con-

A Hindu is free to accept any of a thousand avatars as his personal god. Here three Hindu girls leave a Jain sect temple. The Jains worship peace and abhor any kind of killing.

sidered to be avatars or incarnations of one or another of the
trinity. For example, the popular god Krishna, who delighted in
making love to milkmaids, is supposedly an avatar of Vishnu.
Rama, the supreme hero of the epic poem, *The Ramayana*, is
considered to be the seventh avatar of Vishnu.

Hinduism, unlike other religions, has no basic creed or rituals.
A Hindu is free to accept any (or none at all) of the thousands of
avatars of the trinity as his personal god. Many believe in a god
for every activity and pray to numerous ones. It is not a congre-
gational religion. The Hindu worships alone or with his family. A
basic concept of this religion is that the world is an illusion. Man
is destined to live on earth until he reaches the state where he
becomes aware of the true reality of God. This means he may die
and be born, again and again, until he reaches the state of en-
lightment known as *moksha* by the Hindus and *nirvana* by the
Buddhists. (Buddhism is a reformed outgrowth of Hinduism.) It
is believed that the soul of man attains a mystical union with God
and becomes part of the universe. In his worldly life the Hindu is
bound by *karma* (pronounced *kurma*).

Westerners might call karma fate, for it sums up the belief that
every act and even thought of a person's life sets up a cause and
effect that creates consequences for which he must pay in this or
a future life. In a future life, the Hindu may be born to a higher
position—a king even—or to a lower level, perhaps as an animal,
depending upon his karma and how he conducted himself in his
previous life. The only way he can escape this continual turning
around and around on the wheel of fate is through *moksha*.

One way to escape one's karma is through the philosophy of
yoga—despite American dictionaries to the contrary, the final a is
silent and the word is pronounced yog'. There are five different
varieties of yoga in common practice, and each provides a path to
attaining *moksha*. They are:

- BHAKTI—achieving moksha through love and devotion.
- JNANA—uniting with God through knowledge.

· KARMA—achieving eternal bliss through good deeds and
service.
· RAJA—uniting with God through concentration and will
power.
· HATHA—physical discipline of one's body.

This basic varieties of yoga may take odd and unusual forms.
The penitent who lies on a bed of nails, or otherwise mortifies his
flesh (as one sees so often in books about India), is practicing his
own form of Hatha.

Overshadowing the Hindu's life is something else called
Dharma. There is no exact word in English that means the same
thing, but the Reverend Charles Francis Potter, in *Faiths Men
Live By*, said of it, "It means the way things are and ought to be.
When a Westerner says that certain things 'just aren't done,' a
Hindu would say that to do such things would 'break Dharma.'"
Dharma is what keeps the Hindu bound to the caste system. The
four castes are: Brahman or priestly; Kshatriya or warrior; Vaisya
or merchant-farmer; and Sudra or laboring class. Below these
castes are the Untouchables—the social outcastes—a term which
is no longer in official favor. They are now known as Scheduled
Caste, but their unfortunate situation at the cellar of the caste
system has not improved much.

The caste system has been one of the sources of trouble between the Hindu and Moslem Indians. Another source is the
Hindu's veneration of the cow. Just how and why the cow became sacred to the Hindu religion has been lost in the mists of
time. But as meat eaters and cow killers the Moslems are looked
upon with hatred by the Hindus. The followers of Islam, in turn,
consider the Hindus heretics and a natural enemy.

Although one of the basic tenets of Hinduism is that no life will
be taken for any reason, be it human, animal, or insect, this has
not prevented the Hindus from killing in war. It did not prevent
the royal courts from being the scene of countless murders and
battles to the death over the various thrones of the Hindu states.

One of these struggles was in progress when Alexander the Great defeated Prince Porus in 327 B.C. By defeating local princes and seizing their domains, the Nanda family had built up a vast empire in the Ganges Valley. This Hindu empire was called *Magadha*, and its capital was on the Ganges River, near the present site of Patal in Eastern India. A young man named Chandragupta Maurya became involved in an intrigue to overthrow the Nanda tyrant. He was exposed and forced to flee to the court of Porus. Another story claims he was the illegitimate son of the Nanda king and was exiled for trying to assassinate his father.

Chandragupta met Alexander after the battle with Porus and offered to guide the Macedonians in an attack on the rich Hindu nation. Alexander was delighted, but his war-weary army mutinied. This forced Alexander to turn back, making his return trip down the Indus and then across Persia to Babylon where he died. Chandragupta then attached himself to the court of King Porus.

Alexander left native kings in command of all his conquered Pakistan provinces, but made them subservient to Greek generals. When word was received from Babylon that Alexander was dead, the local kings began to revolt. The Greek generals left by Alexander were involved in a power struggle among themselves and could do nothing to put down the uprisings. Sind established its independence under a Hindu prince. Then, in the Punjab, Chandragupta suddenly appeared as leader of a big army. No record survives as to how he got command of so many troops. The assumption is that he treacherously killed King Porus and usurped the throne of Paurava. Chandragupta drove out the surviving Greeks and Macedonians and turned east to capture Magadha. He changed the empire's name to Maurya and extended it from Bengal to the Hindu Kush Mountains, creating the largest kingdom known in India up to that time.

In the meantime, the Macedonian generals had carved up Alexander's empire among themselves. Seleukos Nikator, after several years of fighting his rival, General Antigonos, gained control of Babylon, Persia, and Afghanistan. The long years of fighting with Antigonos had prevented Seleukos from doing anything about Chandragupta, but in 305 B.C. he led an army into Pakistan along the same route he had traveled with Alexander, nearly twenty years before. The ensuing battle was different this time. Chandragupta had either been present at the battle of the Hydaspes, when Alexander outmaneuvered Porus' elephants, or had heard about it from veterans. Seleukos tried to follow Alexander's strategy, but he was defeated. Seleukos and Chandragupta consented to a nonaggression pact. Seleukos agreed to give up all claim to northern Pakistan and Chandragupta agreed not to attack Seleukos' sovereignty in Afghanistan and Bactria.

Chandragupta was a tyrant who lived in constant fear of his life. He never slept twice in the same room, and he surrounded himself with Amazon women warriors who had orders to slay anyone that tried to approach him. But despite all of this, he was an able ruler. He set up committees to handle various government functions, so that no one man could gain too much power.

The entire empire was divided into three provinces, each governed by a viceroy directly responsible to the king. North Pakistan was one province with Taxila as its capital. Sind, in what is now South Pakistan, was not included in the Magadha Empire. It was so barren that Chandragupta did not consider the land worth his efforts. Aware that swift communication was a major key to holding an empire, the king had a network of roads constructed. The most important of these was the Royal Road that ran from Taxila to the capital, a distance of well over 800 miles. Rest houses were built between towns, and a pony express system carried mail on a regular schedule.

Chandragupta combined his original army, which he had taken from Porus, with the Magadha army he had conquered. The resulting force was so powerful that, after Seleukos was defeated, none dared attack him. This brought years of peace that were extremely favorable to trade. Taxila and North Pakistan benefited from the trade caravans that moved from India across the Khyber Pass into Afghanistan and Bactria, and from there to Europe.

Travelers reported that Taxila was a vast treasure house, its

Part of the ruins of Taxila, the great caravan city in the Punjab. Alexander fought here. And so did Genghis Khan, Tamerlane, the Earthshaker, Babur the Tiger, and Ranjit Singh.

bazaars piled high with rich products for sale. Philostratos of Lemnos, writing sometime after this period, left a description of Taxila as the city was in the days of Chandragupta. He wrote: "From the Indus they [the party of Apollonius of Tyre, the subject of Philostratos' book] were conducted to Taxila, a city about the size of Nineveh [the Assyrian city on the Tigris River]. It is walled like a Greek city and the residence of the viceroy. Outside the walls is a shrine hung with pictures on copper tablets representing the feats of Alexander and Porus. The figures are portrayed in a mosaic of silver, gold and oxidized copper, with the weapons in iron. The metals were so ingeniously worked one into the other that the pictures which they formed are comparable to the productions of the most famous Greek artists."

Strabo, the great geographer who wrote in the time of the Roman emperors, Augustus and Tiberius (at the beginning of the Christian era), also described Taxila. "Between the Indus and the Hydaspes is Taxila," he wrote, "a large city and governed by good laws. The surrounding country is thickly peopled and extremely fertile, as the mountains here begin to subside into the plains."

In a later section of his famous *Geography*, Strabo wrote: "On many points the opinions of the Brachmanes (Brahmans) coincide with those of the Greeks, for the Brachmanes say with them that the world was created, and is liable to destruction, that it is of a spheroidal figure, and that the Deity who made and governs it is diffused through all its parts. . . . Concerning generation, the nature of the soul, and many other subjects, they express views similar to those of the Greeks. They wrap up their doctrines about the immortality of the soul and judgment in Hades in Fables after the manner of Plato. This is the account which Megasthenes gives."

Strabo also quoted Megasthenes about "mention of some strange and unusual customs which existed at Taxila."

Those who are unable from poverty to bestow their daughters in marriage, expose them for sale in the market-place in the flower of their age, a crowd being assembled by the sound of shells and drums. When any person steps forward, first the back of the girl as far as the shoulders is uncovered for his examination, and then the parts in front, and if she pleases him and allows herself at the same time to be persuaded, they marry on such terms as can be agreed upon.

This "marriage mart" was a Babylonian custom, and its use in Taxila is additional proof that this caravan city was a mixture of the culture of many races. In other parts of Pakistan and India, no man would have accepted a woman so exposed in public. In addition, Strabo clearly says these girls were selected because they were too poor to afford a dowry. Yet Diodorus disapprovingly observes: "In selecting a bride the Indians care nothing whether she has a dowry, but choose a wife on account of her good looks and other advantages of the outward person."

Strabo also notes that the Taxilians observed both the Persian Zoroastrian custom of exposing the dead to be eaten by vultures and the Hindu custom of suttee in which a widow throws herself upon the funeral pyre of her husband. These statements contradict each other since the dead cannot be placed in the Zoroastrian "Towers of Silence" for the vultures and cremated at the same time. We can only suppose that what he really meant was that Taxila was the home of many races and each preserved its own customs. It was said that, when a man had many wives, only the one who loved him most was permitted to be burned alive with his corpse. This sometimes led to a fight before a local judge who had to rule which woman indeed loved her husband sufficiently to win the honor of dying with him.

Chandragupta died or abdicated in favor of his son, Bindusara, who reigned until 273 B.C., when Chandragupta's grandson Asoka came to the throne of the Maurya Empire. Asoka, a mighty warrior in his youth, greatly extended his empire, but he was later converted to Buddhism. Thereafter, he tried to rule through love and peace.

Buddhism was not a new religion. It was founded by Prince Siddhartha Gautama who was born in 563 B.C. in what is now Nepal. Quite early in life, he became greatly troubled by the sorrows that afflicted mankind. Accordingly, when he was twenty-nine, he renounced his right to his father's throne, left his wife and family, and spent the next six years searching for truth. The revelation Siddhartha sought came to him as he sat meditating under a *bodhi* tree. He then began to preach his new doctrine. Just as Christianity came from Judaism, and Protestantism from Catholicism, Buddhism developed out of Hinduism.

Siddhartha rejected the Hindu trinity and its thousands of avatars, for he recognized no god. However, he did retain the Hindu concept of the wheel of life with its continuing incarnations leading to *moksha*. He called the Hindu *moksha*—that time when a supplicant becomes enlightened and merges with the spirit of creation—by the name *Nirvana*. He partly rejected the Hindu concept of karma, preaching that life is basically unhappy, and that this worldy sorrow is caused by a desire for all things except salvation, goodness, and truth.

Prince Siddhartha became known as Buddha to his followers who were eager to become Buddhas themselves. (Buddha, rooted in a Sanskrit word meaning to be wise, is translated as The Enlightened One.) Although Buddha gained a considerable following in his lifetime and after his death, his religious philosophy was confined to a local sect, until the conversion of Asoka which occurred about 261 B.C. Asoka not only made Buddhism the state religion, but dispatched missionaries to all neighboring countries. The historian, H. G. Rawlinson, wrote: "The histories of Ceylon and Burma, as of Siam, Japan, and Tibet, may be said to begin with the entrance into them of Buddhism; and in these lands it spread far more rapidly and made a far deeper impression than in China with its already ancient civilization."

In Pakistan, Asoka's missionaries made many converts, but Hinduism was so deeply ingrained that the Buddhist teachers did not have the success that Asoka anticipated. The king, however, was scrupulous about religious tolerance. Even though Hinduism was and is basically a tolerant religion, the Hindu Brahmin—the priestly caste—was greatly disturbed. The original Buddhism recognized no priests; consquently, Brahmins were worried about their own caste if Asoka succeeded, as he hoped he would, in converting all the world to Buddhism. Under Hinduism, the Brahmin was a person of extreme importance. He belonged to the highest caste, even above kings and warriors. Indispensable for the many religious rites, he was the only person who could expound the sacred lore to the people. In addition, many Brahmins rose to great power as advisers to the various rulers. Under the circumstances, the Brahmins did all they could to stamp out the influence of Buddhism as soon as Asoka died. In fact, the Maurya Empire did not long survive Asoka. The king's insistence on rul-

In the Gandhara period, much of the magnificent sculpture showed a fusion of Indian and Grecian styles, like this head found in North Pakistan.

ing by peace and love was not in tune with the violent times, and his once mighty army was weakened to the point that, after his death, the country became the prey of one invader after another.

The Greeks who had settled in Bactria invaded northern Pakistan on the premise that it belonged to them as the heirs of Alexander the Great. They succeeded in founding a small kingdom that included the plains of Peshawar, the Khyber Pass, and a small area in Afghanistan. It was called Gandhara. This Indo-Greek invasion came about 200 B.C., and it reached its peak about 180 B.C. under Menander, its greatest king, who extended the empire to the Punjab. Although of Bactria Greek descent, the Indo-Greeks were more Hindu than Greek. Menander himself was a Buddhist, and under his influence the Gandhara school of art began. This fused the art of India and Greece, producing images of Buddha in a distinctly Greek style.

Menander's capital, Sagala—identified with modern Sialkot on the Punjab plains near Lahore—was described in contemporary writing as a magnificent trade center. "Wise architects have laid it out, and its people know no oppression, since all their enemies have been put down," one account reads. "Its streets are filled with elephants, horses, carriages and foot-passengers, and crowded with men of all sorts." The writer goes on to say that the shops and bazaars were stuffed with fine cloths and jewels and that "sweet odors exhaled from shops where all sorts of flowers and perfumes were tastefully set out."

The Indo-Greek hold on North Pakistan did not last long. By 130 B.C., it had succumbed to Sakas invaders from Central Asia who set up a capital in historic Taxila, but did not succeed in penetrating into the Sind. The Sakas were part of the Parthia Empire that ruled Persia at this time. A king, known as Gondopharnes by the Greeks, was the last of the Saka rulers. According to tradition, Gondopharnes permitted the Apostle Thomas to teach Christianity at Taxila in 47 A.D. Thomas, one of the best known of the original twelve apostles of Christ, was only in Taxila a short time before he was forced to flee when the Kushans overthrew the Saka nation in 48 A.D. According to H. G. Rawlinson, in his history, *India*, "Gondopharnes is a corruption of the Persian Vindapharna. In the Armenian version of the story, this becomes Gathaspar, from which is derived Gaspar, the name given to the second of the Magi [Persian Zoroasterian priest] who visited the cradle of the infant Jesus."

Saint Thomas, leaving Taxila ahead of the invading Kushans, went down the Indus River to Sind, then to the Malabar Coast of India where he founded a Catholic church in 52 A.D. Twenty years later, he moved to the East Coast. There he was killed by the Brahmins who resented the number of converts he was making among the Hindus.

The Kushans, who came from beyond the Hindu Kush Mountains, established their capital at Purushapura (Peshawar). Later, they added Kashmir to their empire and, for a time, brought Sind under their control, so that they ruled all of what is now Pakistan. The greatest of the Kushan rulers was Kanishka who reigned from about 120 to 162 A.D. Like Asoka, Kanishka was converted to Buddhism, but he was disturbed by so many different sects. When he called a general Buddhist Council to reconcile the differences, delegates came from as far away as China. Instead of reconciling the different Buddhist beliefs, the council led to the formation of a completely new Buddhist sect, Mahayana Buddhism. Where Hinayana Buddhism, the original creed, stressed simplicity, had no priests, and looked upon Buddha simply as a great teacher and an ideal to aspire to, Mahayana Buddhism developed a priesthood that practically deified Buddha and developed a pantheon of gods.

Buddhism now began to absorb features from other religions. This was partly due to Brahmin converts to Buddhism. Their conversion was not always a matter of will, but was frequently done to please a monarch. These Brahmin converts tried to reconcile Hinduism and Buddhism. Of this period Rawlinson says, "When Buddhism became the religion of foreign invaders, it entirely lost its original character. Buddha ceased altogether to be a dead teacher and became a living Savior God, incarnate, like Rama and Krishna, for the salvation of the human race."

Up to this point, Buddhism and Hinduism, while serious rivals, had co-existed peacefully, for the Buddhist kings in Hindustan had all been tolerant men. The religious situation now began to change, and eventually would develop into the frightful religious wars and persecutions that are still very prevalent today. Sometime around 484 A.D.—historical dates of this period are notoriously inexact—the White Huns swept down from Central Asia. First they overran Persia, and then they followed the traditional route of India's invaders by crossing the Sulaiman Mountains into the Peshawar Plains and the Punjab. Although the Hun king, Mihiragula, vengefully destroyed both Hindu and Buddhist temples, he made little impression on the country. In 528 A.D., the rulers of the princely states of India put aside their own wars long enough to band together and defeat Mihiragula, when the Huns tried to move into the rest of India.

The defeat of the Huns led to the rise of the Gupta Empire in India. A Chinese visitor to the court of the Gupta ruler, Harsha, in 630 A.D., shows that the struggle between the Hindu Brahmins and the Buddhists had become more than intellectual. Hiuen Tsang, a Chinese Buddhist on a pilgrimage to India, said that, during one of his audiences with Harsha, a fire broke out at the palace gate. During the disturbance this caused, a man rushed in with a knife and tried to kill the king. When the would-be assassin was overpowered, he confessed that he had been hired by Brahmins to slay Harsha because of the king's support of Buddhism.

Despite the king's support, Hinduism was rapidly developing while Buddhism was losing ground. In time it would almost completely disappear from the land of its birth. Had it not been for the missionaries that Asoka had sent out into the world, Buddhism would have died. However, the victory over Buddhism left Hinduism paramount only for a few centuries. A far more formidable rival was being created in Arabia where an ex-camel driver, named Mohammed, founded the religion of Islam. The nature of these two religions made them natural enemies, and their adherents made the most of it. The crimes against humanity, committed in the name of these two religions, have been among the most barbarous in modern history; nor is this struggle now entirely a footnote in history. As late as 1971, the struggle between the Hindus of India and the Moslems of Pakistan caused the death of close to a million people and drove ten million more into wretched exile. Unfortunately, this latest bloodbath did not solve the age-old problem any more than had the previous struggles, for it still lurks in the subcontinent, awaiting another excuse to flare up again.

CHAPTER 4

The Threat of Islam

His name was Kutam and he was an orphan. He lived first with his grandfather and then with an impoverished uncle. While still a boy, he began to travel with camel trains that plied the trade routes between Mecca, his native city, and other commercial centers in Arabia. It was a hard life. The desert was harsh and the people were more so. In those days, men gave their loyalty to their tribes and worshipped local pagan gods. There was constant warfare between tribes and robbers who lurked along the camel trails.

Intellectually, Kutam was far above his companions. He early developed into a leader, and became a very good, successful caravan master. This brought him to the attention of a rich Meccan widow, named Khadijah, who hired him to run her caravans. Though fifteen years older than Kutam, who was then twenty-five, she took him as her husband. In the years that followed, Kutam drove the camels to Mesopotamia, Syria, Palestine, and even into Egypt. On these trips, Kutam came into contact with the Jewish religion in Palestine and the Christian religion in Syria. All his life, he had been an extremely moral man who was dissatisfied with the animism that passed for religion among the Arabic tribes.

When Kutam was about forty, he became so disenchanted that he withdrew to a cave on Mount Hira. Here he pondered over the stories he had heard of the prophets of Judaism and Christianity. He saw great truths in what they taught, but found them lacking as a whole philosophy. Eventually, he had a vision in which the Archangel Gabriel appeared and called upon Kutam to be a prophet and to take the true word of God to his countrymen. A man of integrity, Kutam refused to believe that he had really had a vision from God. However, Khadijah believed that her husband had been chosen by heaven. Kutam disagreed until later, when he had a second vision in which Gabriel once again appeared. This time the angel ordered him to spread the true word of God.

He was still hesitant and at first confined his preaching only to small groups in his own home. But his following increased and he now began to preach in the streets of Mecca where he became known as Mohammed which means the "praised one." He wrote nothing himself, but his followers committed to memory and notes the things he said and revealed to them. In time these were collected into the *Koran*, the sacred book of Islam whose meaning is "submission."

Islam, as developed by Mohammed, is based upon Judaism and Christianity. It has taken many of the characters and stories of both the Old and New Testaments. However, they have been altered to Mohammed's concept of God. Islam teaches that there is but one God who is all-powerful and all-merciful. This God, Allah, wishes man to repent his sins, so he sends prophets to earth to teach man to do his duty to God and his fellow-man. Life on earth is a testing process to determine man's suitability for heaven. During this life on earth, each man is watched by recording angels who note his every good deed and bad. These record books, delivered to each man on Judgment Day, determine if he should go to heaven or hell.

A Moslem has five duties under the law of the Koran. One is a requirement to pray five times a day between dawn and nightfall. He is required to give alms to charity; to repeat the *Kalimah* creed: "There is no God but Allah and Mohammed is His Prophet"; to fast during the daylight hours of the month of Ramadan (ninth month of the Muslim calendar); and, if at all possible, to make a pilgrimage to the holy city of Mecca.

Islam, a very moral and rigidly strict religion, denounces usury,

The national Islamic mosque in Islamabad, the nation's capital.

gambling, and strong drink. Some of the things Mohammed taught brought him into conflict with men in Mecca. He had to flee with his followers to Yathrib (now Medina). There he was well received and developed a strong following. When Mecca declared war on Medina, Mohammed was able to defeat his enemies and march in triumph into Mecca in 630 A.D. Two years later, he succeeded in bringing almost all of Arabia under Islam. He died shortly thereafter.

Islam is a militant religion, and soon after Mohammed's death his followers launched a *jihad*—holy war—that extended the Arabian Empire to Iraq, Persia, Palestine, North Africa, and Spain. Arabic sailors first introduced the Islamic religion to Pakistan a few years after Mohammed's death. They came through the Persian gulf and across the Arabian Sea to the ports of Sind. At that time, most of Pakistan was no longer dominated by India. Kashmir was the powerful nation and Taxila, the ancient caravan trade center in the Punjab, was a vassal state to the Kashmiri king. The Punjab around Multan, where Alexander the Great had nearly been killed, was a separate, independent state. In the south, Sind was a powerful state that also controlled Baluchistan. In 644 A.D., Arabs invaded Baluchistan and, in 710, finally killed the Buddhist King of Sind, annexing his state. The Arab conquest of Sind changed the country from Buddhist to Islamic, but it did not affect the rest of Pakistan or India. Although the Arabs of Sind made border raids, they never constituted a threat to the rest of Pakistan. The final triumph of Islam in Pakistan, hundreds of years later, was due to the Turks and the Mongols.

The Turks came from Afghanistan where an ex-Turki slave, named Sabuktigin, had created a kingdom at Ghazni below the present site of Kabul. He soon began to make raids across the Khyber Pass. The local Hindu king, Jaipal, was unable to stop the raids. He asked help from the various Rajput princes who ruled the divided states of North India. This Hindu confederacy was disastrously defeated on the plains of Peshawar in 991 A.D. Sabuktigin was a raider rather than a conqueror. He struck and then retreated with his loot back to Ghazni. He died in 997 and was succeeded by his son, the famous Mahmud of Ghazni, who followed his father's war trail. Each fall, Mahmud led his hordes deep into Pakistan and then into India. When hot weather returned in the spring, he marched back to Ghazni with his booty.

Mahmud considered these raids not only as a source of ready treasure, but as a holy war against infidels. He smashed Hindu and Buddhist temples, wrecked images of their gods, and slaughtered their priests. Thus he built the foundation for the bitter struggle between Hinduism and Islam that continues to this very day. An Afghan historian left this record of Mahmud's treatment of the Hindus he captured: "That enemy of Allah, Jaipal, and his children and grandchildren and relations were bound with ropes and dragged before the Sultan. They were evildoers on whose faces the fumes of infidelity were evident." The writer went on to tell how the prisoners were driven along by blows, and how Mahmud stripped millions in jewels from the bodies of his many captives. "Allah bestowed upon His friends such an amount of booty as was beyond all bounds and calculations, including 500 thousand Hindu slaves."

The frightened princes of the Hindu Rajput kingdoms of North India tried to form another confederation against Mahmud. As before, they were too suspicious of each other to cooperate properly, and Mahmud defeated them easily before returning to Ghazni at the end of the fighting season.

In the winter of 1023, Mahmud led his army down the Indus. Multan surrendered without a fight, and Mahmud marched on to the Arabian Sea in Sind. Here he turned down the coast, circling the Rann of Kutch, and attacked the ancient Indian city of Somnath. This city was famous for a magnificent temple dedicated to Shiva. The object of worship in the temple was a nine-and-a-half foot representation of Shiva in his role of giver of life. This was a stone *lingam*—the male sexual organ. The image was surrounded by solid gold bells, backed by veils set in precious stones. A thousand Brahmins ministered to it, bathing the image daily in waters carried a thousand miles from the sacred Ganges River. The temple's upkeep required taxes from ten thousand villages.

The defenders of Sommath fought valiantly, but the Turks scaled the walls. The Hindus took refuge in the temple, praying to Shiva for help against the invaders. Mahmud pressed in on them, slaughtering 50,000 Hindus in the final assault. When the battle was over he gave orders for his troops to destroy the image of Shiva because the Moslem religion forbids any representation —statue or painting—of gods or man. Those who permit images in their temples and churches are idolators in the eyes of orthodox Moslems. When Mahmud, in accordance with Moslem beliefs, ordered the sacred *lingam* destroyed, a delegation of Brahmins petitioned him to spare their god. They promised to ransom the image with an amount, they assured Mahmud, far greater than he had received from sacking the city. This would be accomplished by collecting donations from all in India who worshipped Shiva. He refused, saying, "How can I appear before Allah on Judgment Day if I spare an idol?" The image was broken into pieces and buried at the door of the temple which Mahmud turned into a Moslem mosque. Thus the feet of the "true believers" would forever tramp on the grave of the heathen god.

After Mahmud died in 1030, his empire was overwhelmed by the Afghans of Ghor, and the remnants of Mahmud's people fled from Ghazni to Lahore. After Mahmud's death, the Rajputs of India enjoyed a respite for fifty years. Then the Afghans of Ghor produced their greatest king, Muhammad Ghori. He raided Pakistan and India every winter as Mahmud had done, looting, destroying Hindu temples, and slaughtering unbelievers. His viceroy, Kutb-ud-din Ibak, later formed the "Slave Kings" dynasty and extended the Moslem Empire to Delhi. For a time, at the beginning of the 13th century, it appeared that the bloody Mongol conqueror Genghis Khan would sweep over India. After crossing the Khyber Pass—traditional entry for invaders—the Mongol horde penetrated as far as Peshawar, then turned back to plunder western Asia.

Pakistan and India were not so fortunate when Tamerlane, the Earthshaker (Timur the Lame), invaded Pakistan in 1398. He swept through Peshawar, Taxila, and the Punjab and went on to capture Delhi, the capital of North India. Tamerlane, in his autobiography, said that he invaded India in part to make war on the infidels and in part to plunder. But India was then under Moslem control, and actually he fought men of his own religion. He did, however, kill more than his share of Hindus. A contemporary report stated: "Towers were built high with their [Hindus] heads." No other conqueror of India spilled so much blood. When he left Delhi, the city was so devastated that legend claims that not even a bird flew over the ruins for two months.

Tamerlane withdrew to terrorize Central Asia, but he left a lieutenant, Khizr Khan, to hold his conquered territory east of the Indus. After Khizr died, other members of his family ruled until surplanted by a Pathan, named Bahlol, who established the Lodi dynasty. This family, in turn, was succeeded in the sixteenth century by the Great Moguls who would rule until the coming of the British in the eighteenth century.

These centuries of Moslem domination were bitter and bloody years for the Hindus. Things were not so bad in Pakistan because large numbers of Hindus accepted Islam. One reason for the mass conversions was the great number of low-caste Hindus in the Indus Valley. Hinduism gave them no choice but to remain at their low social level until they died. They could better themselves only by rebirth, and then they might be reincarnated to a still lower level of life for mistakes made in this one. Mohammed, on the other hand, taught that all men are equal. This, coupled with the fact that several of the Turki rulers of India had been slaves before they became kings, deeply impressed the low-caste Indians.

Even so, the bulk of Indians remained Hindu. Pakistan and East Bengal became predominantly Moslem, thus setting the stage for today's troubles. These Moslems were not Arabic, Turki, or Mongol, but were mainly of Hindu origin. They accepted Islam either to escape the rigid caste system of the Hindus, or to avoid the heavy poll taxes some Moslem rulers put on unbelievers. Moslem rulers varied in their treatment of the Hindus, but generally resorted to heavy oppression. In the past, invaders had been absorbed by Hinduism, but the Moslem religion is too rigid to permit such an escape. Ruler after ruler felt it his sacred duty to destroy the enemies of Allah. Mahmud's philosophy was plainly expressed: "Since the inhabitants of this land are chiefly idolators and infidels, by the order of God and His Prophet, it is right for us to conquer them."

Ala-ud-din, who ruled at the end of the thirteenth century, made his own views clear in a statement quoted by the historian, Barani: "The Hindus will never become submissive and obedient until they are reduced to poverty. I have therefore given orders that just enough shall be left to them of corn, milk, and curds, from year to year, that they shall not accumulate hoards and property. To prevent rebellion, in which many would perish, I issue such ordinances as I consider to be for the good of the state and for the benefit of the people. Men are heedless and disobedient to my commands. So I have to be severe to bring them to obedience."

This same attitude governed Moslem kings in India for the next hundred years.

The Moslem oppression of these years hurt India more than it did the regions that now comprise the land of Pakistan. The people here had embraced Islam to a greater extent than those of the rest of India, and as Moslem converts they were treated as Moslems. In fact, Pakistan profited considerably. The caravan cities still enjoyed their rich trade and the rulers, mindful of the need for food, greatly extended the Indus Valley irrigation system.

When not destroying Hindu temples, Firoz Shah was one of the outstanding builders among the Moslem sultans. He is credited with extending the Punjab canal system and building 200 towns, 50 dams and 30 reservoirs, at least half of which were in Pakistan.

It was during this period that Urdu, until recently the national language of Pakistan, developed. Urdu itself means "camp" in Persian and the language Urdu was originally called *Zaban-i-urdu* or "language of the camp." It is a mixture of western Hindi with Arabic and Persian words added. Although Urdu was based upon the Hindu language, it is written in Arabic characters.

The Pathans, who ruled as the Lodi Dynasty after the bloody invasion of Tamerlane, were both the best and the worst of the Moslem rulers of India. Bahlol, who founded the dynasty in 1450, died in 1489. His son, Sikander, ruled during what became known as the "Golden Age" of Moslem India. Sikander particularly favored North Pakistan because so many Pathans still lived in the hills above Peshawar. He apparently had a fetish for honesty. An efficient spy system brought him daily reports of his kingdom. These included local prices and, if there was the slightest indication of profiteering, Sikander immediately dispatched investigators to Peshawar, Taxila, Benares, or wherever the trouble might be. He placed trusted lieutenants in charge of each province and ruled them rather than the people. Each was charged by Sikander to govern according to the best principles of the Koran. Honesty, justice, and piety were the watchwords of his rule. He sincerely wanted the good will of his people and avoided any wars of conquest, although he was quick to defend any encroachment on his own territory. According to one contemporary historian: "A new sort of life obtained, for people high and low were polite, and self-respect, integrity and devotion to religion prevailed, like as had never been in former reigns."

Sikander was one of the few who believed in religious tolerance. Although a strict Moslem himself and untiring in his efforts to win converts, he could understand the need of others to follow the dictates of their own consciences. This is very clearly shown in his treatment of Kabir. Originally a Moslem weaver, Kabir came under the influence of a Hindu guru (teacher) named

Ramananda. From this association Kabir decided that all religious sects were wrong. He said that Arab prayer beads were merely wood, and Hindu idols were nothing but stone. He preached that the common man in the street was nearer to God than any priest. "God is One, whether we worship Him as Allah or Rama," he claimed. "There is one Father of Hindu and Moslems: He is the Lord of all the earth, my Guardian and my Priest."

This first attempt to bring the Hindu and the Moslem religions into a single creed naturally infuriated both orthodox Moslems and Hindu Brahmans alike. Under Sikander, justice was the monopoly of the sultan and all Kabir's enemies could do was appeal to their ruler.

Sikander refused to take action against Kabir, and the prophet continued to preach his religion until his death in 1518. His teachings might have prevented the slaughter of the religious wars ahead, but the Moslem and Hindu religions were too sharply divided ever to be brought together. Even his disciples clung to their individual beliefs, showing by their actions after his death that they had been followers of the guru, but not believers in his visions. This attitude was clearly revealed at his burial. According to the story of his funeral, both Kabir's Moslem and Hindu followers demanded the right to bury their teacher. The quarrel between them reached such a heated point that the spirit of the dead man supposedly appeared and ordered them to raise the shroud from his corpse. They did so and found that the body had vanished. In its place they found scattered roses. The flowers were divided equally between the Hindus and the Moslems. It is said that the division was so exact that one extra petal had to be split in half to insure this exactness. The Moslem followers of Kabir then buried their half of the roses in accordance with Moslem beliefs. The Hindus took the remaining half, burned them as Hindu dogma required, and scattered the ashes on the waters of the sacred Ganges River.

Under Bahlol Lodi, the Pathan Empire extended from the

Sulaiman Mountains that separated Pakistan from Afghanistan to the Plains of Delhi. The empire began to crumble under Bahlol's grandson, Ibrahim Lodi, a despot who believed in the divine right of kings. An intolerant tyrant, he not only offended his Hindu subjects, but the proud Afghan Pathans upon whom his power rested. In the Punjab the Viceroy of Lahore, Daulat Khan, refused to acknowledge the sovereignty of Ibrahim Lodi. Sind, in South Pakistan, was also independent. At first, Ibrahim was too busy with other revolts in North India to do anything about the independence of the Punjab. But as he gradually stamped out revolts in India, it became only a matter of time before his armies would invade the Punjab. Daulat Khan knew that he could not defeat the royal armies, so he started to look for an ally to help him in the coming struggle with Ibrahim Lodi. The ally he found was Babur the Tiger, first of the Great Moguls.

5

The Great Moguls

Mogul means Mongol, but by a peculiarity of history the Great Mogul Babur was not a Mongol at all. He was from Turkestan and became ruler of a small principality there, when his father died. Babur was then eleven years and four months old. He was the fifth descendent of Timur the Lame through his father's bloodline and the fourteenth descendent of the mighty Mongol conqueror, Genghis Khan, on his mother's side. As soon as he became king of Farghana, the small Turkestan principality, he was attacked by two uncles who ruled adjoining kingdoms. Babur successfully beat back the attacks and gained such experience at war that he began his own conquests, when he was only fifteen. He had grown up on tales of his great ancestors and was determined to follow their example.

Samarkand had been Timur's capital. Its capture now became the goal of Babur's life. When Babur's uncle, who was King of Samarkand, died in 1494, the ruler's sons began to fight over the empty throne. Seeking to take advantage of his cousins' warfare, Babur attacked Samarkand in 1496. He was repulsed, but came back to take the "golden city" the next year. Disaster struck immediately. The sixteen-year-old conqueror became dangerously ill with a fever whereupon revolts broke out, both in conquered Samarkand and in Babur's native province of Farghana. Instead of being lord of an empire, Babur suddenly became a homeless fugitive who had to hide in the hills to escape death. Although Babur said, in his beautifully written diary, that he cried "a little," he was not daunted. He regathered his army and twice again captured Farghana and Samarkand, only to be driven out as he had been the first time.

All this happened before he was twenty-one years old. During those eventful years, Babur often starved and his band of followers dropped to less than three hundred. Yet it was said that his good spirits never wavered nor did his belief in his ultimate destiny to rule over all the land once conquered by his famous ancestor, Genghis Khan. But in time he realized that his relatives were too strongly entrenched in Turkestan. Accordingly, he turned to Afghanistan and conquered Kabul. He was dispossessed from there twice before he could make his conquest permanent. Then Babur tells us in his diary: "From the year 1504, when I obtained the principality of Kabul, I had never ceased to think of the conquest of Hindustan. But I had never found a suitable opportunity."

Before beginning the actual conquest of India, Babur made three raids into Pakistan. These were made each year because the stubborn hillmen of the Khyber Pass region only paid their tribute to the throne at the point of a sword. These raids also served to acquaint his soldiers with conditions in the Indus Valley. Then, in 1519, Babur began his drive along the route taken by Genghis Khan. Aided by cannon and muskets, the first ever used in India, he easily swept across the Peshawar Plains, crossed the Indus, and captured Bajaur on the Jhelum River. With northern Punjab in his grasp, he sent a messenger to Ibrahim Lodi in Delhi, demanding that he cede all the Punjab to Babur. "It is mine by historic right," he said, "for it was conquered by my ancestor, Genghis Khan."

Unfortunately for Babur, trouble arose in Afghanistan. He was forced to return, able to leave only a lieutenant in charge of his Punjab conquests. The Punjabi ran him out as soon as Babur was gone, but found themselves again facing the angry conqueror the next year. The Punjab, at this time, was divided. The southern area was a separate principality ruled by Daulat Khan from Lahore. Although nominally a vassal of Ibrahim Lodi, the Lord of Delhi, Daulat had practically made his Lahore province independent. Then Ibrahim Lodi successfully concluded his wars with his Hindu neighbors in the Deccan Plateau of India and now was free to punish Daulat Khan. Daulat was frightened and sent word to Babur that he was ready to join Babur in a war on Delhi. All he asked in return was to be confirmed as ruler of Lahore under Babur.

Babur began to march, but unfortunately for Daulat Khan it was farther from Kabul to Lahore than from Delhi to Lahore. Ibrahim Lodi got to Pakistan first. When Babur crossed the Indus, he found that Ibrahim had taken Lahore and that Daulat Khan had fled for his life. Babur defeated Ibrahim in the battle for Lahore, but prudently did not pursue the defeated Lodi king into India. Daulat now came out of hiding, but was disappointed when Babur refused to restore him to the throne of Lahore. Instead, he was given a smaller Punjab principality. During the next two years, North Pakistan seethed with intrigue, as different petty rulers maneuvered for position. Daulat betrayed Babur and seized three principalities. Then, Alam Khan, whom Babur had sent to help rule the Punjab, decided that Daulat Khan was the man of the hour. He deserted Babur and joined Daulat in an attack on Delhi. When they were badly defeated, Babur crossed the Khyber Pass, determined not only to reconquer North Pakistan, but to go all the way to Delhi this time. He smashed through the Punjab. Daulat took refuge in a fortress, but Babur stormed the walls. Daulat was captured and dragged before the angry Mogul and when Daulat was slow to bow, Babur had his captive's legs kicked out from under him. Babur then ordered Daulat sent back to prison near Peshawar, but the captive died on the way.

Babur then swept on across the Punjab into India where he defeated Ibrahim Lodi at the Battle of Panipat near Agra. This decisive battle destroyed the Lodi Dynasty. It was succeeded by the Mogul Dynasty that would—except for a fifteen-year break— rule both India and Pakistan for the next two hundred years.

After the conquest of Delhi made him master of North India, Babur suddenly found himself in the same position as Alexander the Great. His troops wanted to go home. They were hillmen who hated the hot summer plains of India. In his autobiography, Babur wrote:

> I told them that empire and conquest could not exist without the material and means of war; that royalty and nobility could not exist without subjects and dependent provinces; that after undertaking great hardships and exposing ourselves to battle and bloodshed, by the Divine favor I had routed my formidable enemy. And now what hardships oblige us to abandon our conquests? I said let every one who calls himself my friend never henceforward make such a proposal; but if there be among you any who cannot bring himself to stay with me, let him depart.

After this speech, only two soldiers in all the thousands among his troops accepted Babur's offer to leave. Babur spent the rest of his life in battle to protect his empire. According to legend, Babur became distraught when his beloved son Humayun became deathly ill. He consulted a seer who told him that the prince would not recover unless he gave away the single thing he loved

Elaborate tombs in the Sind Desert recall the Mogul period in Pakistan's history.

most. "He loves me best," the king replied. He walked around his son's bed, crying to heaven to allow him to absorb Humayun's illness. From that moment on, according to the legend, the prince began to improve, but three months later, in December 1530, Babur was dead.

Humayun was brave, but he lacked his father's decisiveness and military genius. Worse yet, he placed too much trust in his faithless relatives and friends. They betrayed him, time and again, so that eventually their defection and his own poor generalship lost Humayun the great empire his father had won. When his army collapsed in a battle with Sher Kahn, an Afghan king from the province of Bibar, Humayan fled to Pakistan. For the next five years, he went from one principality to another, futilely seeking aid and fighting as best he could with his constantly dwindling forces.

He was unable to make any headway in the Punjab, so he attacked Sind which was then broken into several principalities ruled by various rajahs. While in lower Sind, Humayun happened to notice the beautiful fourteen-year-old daughter of the spiritual adviser to Humayun's brother, Hindel. When he announced that he would marry her, Hindel was outraged and said that he looked upon the girl as their sister. Actually, it appears that Hindel had designs upon her himself. Her father was displeased, for he did not think that Humayun had much of a future. The girl, Hamida Banu, was even more displeased. "He is too big!" she cried. "Even when I stand on tiptoes, I can scarcely reach high enough to touch his collar."

The king was infatuated and was not concerned with her smallness or his largeness, or with the disapproval of his brother or her father. And so they were married and she became his second queen. Under Moslem law, he was permitted four wives. He had already married three women, but two had been killed in the war with Sher Kahn.

The siege in lower Sind failed soon after his marriage and Humayun had to retreat again. He and his army nearly perished in crossing the Sind Desert during the hottest part of the year. Finally he received help from the rajah of a small principality. Leaving his wives here, Humayun resumed his march. He was camped in the desert when a messenger arrived on October 20, 1542, with news that Hamida Banu had given birth to a son. Humayun wept, both from joy and sorrow—joy at the birth of an heir and sorrow because his destitution prevented him from giving rich presents to his followers, as custom demanded. He broke up a piece of musk and passed out bits to his nobles. "Some day," he said, "my son will fill the world as this perfume fills my tent." And it happened as he predicted, for the son was Akbar, most remarkable of all the Mogul rulers.

Shortly afterward, a Sind rajah gave Humayun money and supplies in order to get him out of Sind. Humayun promptly headed for Kandahar in Afghanistan where his two brothers, Kamran and Askari, were in control. They met him with an army, forcing the outcast king to flee to Persia. The Shah of Persia gave him aid in return for Humayun's promise to convert from orthodox Islam to the Shia sect, a sect which had split away from orthodox Islam soon after Mohammed's death in a quarrel over dogma. Humayun also agreed to force Shiism on all people he conquered. This Persian help permitted Humayun to defeat his brothers and after much fighting he became king of Kabul in Afghanistan. This was the base city used by Babur, first of the great Moguls, to conquer India.

In India, Sher Kahn ruled justly and ably, but he was already old when he stole the throne from Humayun. He died in May, 1545, and the Afghan nobles began a power struggle to succeed him. None had the strength to subdue the others, so the country was split into principalities, with each rival getting his share. Sind in South Pakistan remained independent, but the north was split into two practically autonomous provinces. However, this arrangement did not satisfy the greedy Afghan princes. They kept fighting among themselves, which gave Humayun the opportunity to cross the Indus with an army from Kabul. He quickly captured Lahore and then all of the Punjab. The climax of the fighting came on June 22, 1555, when he recaptured Delhi to complete the reconquest of his original kingdom. This victory was made possible by division among the Afghan successors to Sher Kahn rather than by Humayun's military ability. As a military leader, he was mediocre. This time the Moguls returned to Delhi to stay until ousted by the British in the eighteenth century.

Soon after his victory, Humayun died from slipping on the stairs while on his way to prayer. His death was concealed and a servant, wearing his royal robes, appeared each morning in the audience window in order to assure the people that the king lived. The subterfuge continued until courtiers were able to insure the succession of thirteen-year-old Akbar. The boy had been made viceroy of Lahore by his father and was in the Punjab at the time of his father's death. He was hurriedly brought back in secret and coronated before his uncles, who had hoped to steal the throne for themselves, learned that Humayun was dead.

Akbar became king on February 11, 1556. The first part of his reign was turbulent because the Hindus made a very determined effort to drive the Moguls out of India and at one point actually succeeded in recapturing Delhi for the first time in 350 years. In the end, Akbar, after years of fighting, extended his empire from the Bay of Bengal, in the east, almost to the Persian border in Afghanistan. He then conquered a large section of South India, Baluchistan, and all of Sind, comprising the largest Indian empire to be ruled up to this time.

In May, 1578, Akbar underwent a spiritual crisis. He felt inadequate to face life after death. However, this was nothing particularly new. He had undergone a personal spiritual crisis when he was fourteen, and ever after had thought a great deal about religion. When he was twenty, in 1562, he had abolished most of the restrictions upon the Hindus and their religion. Akbar had done this, even though he was a devout Sunni Moslem who faithfully said his five prayers each day. But as time went by, he became increasingly concerned about the discrepancies and inconsistencies he saw in the religion of Islam. In 1575, in order to clear his mind of these growing doubts, Akbar built the *Ibadat Khana*—House of Worship—at Fatehpur Sikri. Here, each Thursday evening, he brought together the foremost thinkers from each of the conflicting Moslem sects to explain their views in open meetings.

The arguments in the *Ibadat Khana* only served to reveal the intolerance of the different members who openly quarreled with one another. One sect leader called another "an accursed wretch" and tried to strike another with his staff. Once the wrangling became so bitter that a historian recorded that "a horrid noise and confusion ensued. His Majesty became very angry at the rude behavior of those he had summoned to speak about God."

These intolerant outbursts further disillusioned the king about the Moslem religion. "Why should truth," he asked, "be confined to one religion or creed like Islam which is comparatively new and scarcely a thousand years old?" As a result, Akbar now turned to other religions, not to seek out one he could follow, but to hunt for the best elements in each. The "essence of the rose," he called it. This essence he intended to weave into a new religion.

The idea of a universal religion that encompassed the best of all creeds was nothing new in India. Kabir had tried to blend what were to him the better elements of the Hindu and Moslem religions in the days of Babur. A contemporary of Kabir's, although a much younger man, was the guru, Nanak, who founded Sikhism, the religion of the famous Sikhs of the Punjab. Nanak also taught that Allah and the Hindu pantheon were one and the same. In time the peaceful religion of Nanak would change into a militant creed for a warrior race, but in Akbar's era it was still an attempt to bridge what Nanak thought to be the best of two religions.

So in the spirit of Kabir and Nanak, although differing from them in beliefs, Akbar began a personal crusade to determine what was best in all the religions of his time. At Akbar's invitation, divines of Sikhism, Hinduism, Zoroasterism, Buddhism, and finally Christianity came to speak and argue in the House of Worship. It is significant that Akbar had little to do with the teachers of the Moslem religion. Late in his life, Akbar wrote:

"Formerly I persecuted men in conformity with my faith and deemed it Islam. As I grew in knowledge, I was overwhelmed with shame. What constancy is to be expected from proselytes on compulsion? If men walk in the way of God's will, interference with them would be in itself reprehensible; if otherwise, they are under the malady of ignorance and deserve my compassion.

This complete tolerance was unique in the world of Akbar's day. In Europe, the Catholic Inquisition was bloodily stamping out what it considered to be heresy. In the rest of India, the Brahmans were ruthlessly suppressing threats to the Hindu religion. In the Middle East, Islam tolerated no competition; nor were Akbar's subjects pleased by their monarch's religious tolerance. While the Hindus rejoiced over the removal of the stiff taxes that previous Moslem kings had imposed upon their religious practices (including a tax for throwing the ashes of their dead in the sacred ·Ganges River), they were infuriated when Akbar abolished their cherished practices, such as child marriage and suttee. The Hindus also resented Akbar's refusal to stop the Moslems from killing the cattle which the Hindus held sacred.

The Moslems, on the other hand, detested the Hindus for eating pork and for failing to circumcise their children. They considered the king a backsliding heretic for not destroying Hindu temples, as his predecessors had done. The foreign religious figures whom Akbar entertained were not happy with the monarch, either. However, Akbar was genuinely interested in their various religions and his questions convinced each one that the king was on the verge of accepting his particular creed. The Jesuit priests, Fathers Ridolfo Aquaviva and Anthony Monserrate, at one time wrote glowing letters back to Rome predicting that Akbar would soon convert to Catholicism. They eventually departed in disillusionment, realizing that the king had no intention of embracing anyone's religion.

Akbar finally announced his purpose in 1582. It was to determine those things he felt were best in each religion and mold them into a creed of his own. The exact details of this religion were not recorded. However, Abul Fazl, who wrote the history of Akbar's reign and was a personal favorite of the king, said: "It had the great advantage of not losing what is good in one religion while gaining whatever is better in the other." It appears that he built upon the basis of Islam, but rejected the idea of a Judgment Day which Mohammad had taken from Judaism and Christianity. He then added so much of Hinduism that followers of that religion believe he could have been converted to that creed if the Brahmans could have been induced to give up their multiplicity of gods and idols. Among the Hindu beliefs Akbar absorbed were the sacredness of cattle and transmigration of souls. From Zoroasterism, the ancient Persian religion, he placed God in the sun and in evening devotions, when the sun had set, Akbar prostrated himself before a sacred fire which symbolized the sun. However, he did not accept Azura-Mazda, the Persian sun god. His concept of God seems to have been closer to the Buddhist concept of Nirvana where the supplicant, finally obtaining relief from the wheel of rebirths, enters and becomes part of the Spirit of the Universe. Akbar once said: "Each man according to his condition and beliefs give the Supreme Being a Name, but in reality to name the Unknowable is vain."

Din Ilahi—the Divine Faith, as Akbar called his personal religion—attracted few disciples outside the royal court. And after Akbar's death, in 1605, it died quickly. *Din Ilahi* is itself of little historical importance in the history of the world, for it was never accepted beyond a few people immediately surrounding the king. However, Akbar stands above other religious reformers in that he earnestly tried to bring about order out of the world's religious chaos. He was the first king to insist that his subjects had the right to determine their own individual ways to salvation. In his own view of religion, he refused to depend upon blind faith and the preachings of priests and teachers. He listened to all with courtesy and genuine interest and he tried to apply reason to the great conflicts that he found among the different creeds. But never once did he try to force his own beliefs upon others. Although a strict believer in a single God, he still permitted the Hindus to rebuild temples dedicated to their pantheon.

Although in every respect Akbar was a great king, he was deeply hated in Pakistan. In the nearly 900 years, since the Arabian sailors first introduced the Moslem religion to the port cities of Sind, Islam had become the predominant religion of the Indus Valley. Then Akbar tried to unify his country and its people. He sought to give them tolerance and proposed something that neither the Moslems nor the Hindus wanted. And so the chance to avoid the bloody religious conflicts of the future died with Akbar the Great.

6

From Moguls to the British

Akbar's successor was his son, Jahangir, who was a drunkard and an opium eater. Like his father, Jahangir distrusted Islam. He flirted with Christianity for a while, but as he sank deeper into an alcoholic and narcotic stupor, he took less and less interest in any religion. He died in 1628 and was succeeded by his son, Shah Jahan. Three years after Shah Jahan became ruler, his beloved wife, Mumtaz Mahal, died. The grief-stricken king built the magnificent Taj Mahal at Agra, India, in her memory.

Shah Jahan was a bigoted Moslem who believed that suppression of the Hindu religion was a sacred duty. Since the people of Pakistan are predominantly Moslem, they did not suffer under Shah Jahan as did the Hindus, but Pakistan did become a battlefield for his sons during Shah Jahan's last years. Even before the aging king died, his four sons fought among themselves for the right to succeed him. Two were weak and dropped out of the fight. The remaining two, Dara Shikok and Aurangzeb, massed armies and went to war.

Dara Shikok, the king's favorite, lost the war. He fled to the Punjab where he had been viceroy prior to the civil war. The frightened Punjabis, fearing Aurangzeb's wrath, locked the gates of Lahore against Dara Shikok and his few remaining followers. In despair the prince started across the Sind Desert where his beloved wife died from lack of water. Dara's only hope was to get to Afghanistan where so many previous attacks on Pakistan and India had been staged. A Baluchistan rajah, an old friend of Dara's, offered to guide the fugitives through the mountains into Afghanistan. Instead, he sold them to Aurangzeg.

Francois Bernier, a French physician who wrote *Travels in the Mogul Empire* in 1670, saw Dara in captivity and left this description:

> He was seated on a miserable, worn-out elephant covered with filth. He no longer wore the necklace of large pearls that was the badge of a prince of Hindustan. His rich turban and embroidered coat were gone. He and his son Siphir wore dirty cloth of the coarsest texture. His turban was a Kashmir shawl resembling that worn by the poorest people. In this appearance Dara and his son were led through the bazaars and every quarter of the city of Lahore on his way to captivity in Delhi.

Shortly thereafter, assassins murdered Dara Shikok and his son. Dara's head was carried to Aurangzeb in Delhi where the blood was washed off in the conqueror's presence, so he could assure himself that his brother and rival was truly dead. Aurangzeb began to cry. "Let this shocking sight no more offend my eyes," he declared. "Take his head and bury it in Humayun's tomb."

Later, Aurangzeb hunted down Dara's remaining son and had him poisoned while in the state prison. Then, in 1659, he imprisoned his aged father, Shah Jahan, in the Red Fort in Agra. The old emperor was given everything he asked for in captivity, except freedom. He spent his last days at the window of his palatial prison, looking out at the Taj Mahal, the world-famous structure he had built to immortalize his love for the dead Mumtaz Mahal.

Aurangzeb was an orthodox Moslem, stern and puritanical in his religion. He immediately began a systematic program to destroy Hinduism, undoing all the good that previous rulers had accomplished in trying to bring the two races and religions closer together. To be sure, some Moslem kings had oppressed the Hindus, but Aurangzeb went beyond what any of his predecessors had done. He ordered all temples destroyed. He suppressed all schools "teaching the practice of this infidel religion." He even invaded the sacred Hindu city of Benares which other kings had avoided, fearful of causing a Hindu uprising. The great temple of Visvanath was destroyed and a Moslem mosque erected on its site. Towns that bore names of Hindu gods were renamed. Hindu clerks were dismissed from government service. A 5 per cent tax was placed on all goods imported by Hindus. Moslem merchants, however, were exempted from this tax. The old poll tax, requiring each Hindu to pay a special tax just for the right to exist, was revived.

This tyranny led to revolts and disorders which Aurangzeb put down with a bloody hand. On one occasion, Hindu demonstrators blocked the king's road, as he was on his way to a mosque to worship. Soldiers charged forward to disperse them, but the king waved them back. Aurangzeb wanted an example that would spread terror throughout the land. He had war elephants brought up and sent them charging through the tightly packed mass of humanity, trampling a blood path for the king's entourage. Contemporary Hindu writers likened the terror to "the day of Judgment."

In Pakistan, the Hindu element was just as poorly treated, but disturbances were minor because of the small number of Hindus. However, Aurangzeb's tyranny did have a profound effect in that

In the wild hill country, constantly plagued by wars and bandits, the villagers built walled enclosures on hilltops for easier defense.

it destroyed all hope of establishing any rapport between the two religions. Moreover, it directly led to vicious oppression of the Moslems, after the British seized control of India and favored the Hindus. It also led to the demand for a separate Hindu and Moslem India, resulting in the eventual formation of the nation of Pakistan.

After Aurangzeb put the Hindus in their place, the Moslem community found that their new emperor intended them to pay more than lip service to their religion. He set up a system of public spies to insure that there was no drinking, gambling, or prostitution, as the Koran decrees. The spies also checked to see that everyone prayed five times each day, their faces turned toward Mecca, and that they ate nothing during the daylight hours of the month-long fast of Ramadan. Nonorthodox Moslem sects were persecuted as severely as the Hindus.

The hill tribes of northwest Pakistan gave Aurangzeb considerable trouble, for they lived by plundering caravans and towns in the valleys. The king fought a number of indecisive local wars. Finally, he had to resort to bribes and guile to keep open the caravan trade routes through the Khyber Pass. He paid off local chiefs and then used spies to stir up rivalry and jealousy among them. This prevented the proudly independent chieftains from banding together against the king.

Then, in the Punjab, Aurangzeb attempted to destroy Sikhism which had become widespread there. Instead, he succeeded in turning Sikhism from a gentle religion that attempted to find a middle ground between Hinduism and Islam into a fanatical warrior sect. This change would eventually cause two bloody wars between the Sikhs and the British and would divide the Punjab between Pakistan and India in 1947. The result of this partition was that millions of people were uprooted and the atrocities of the twentieth century equaled those of the Middle Ages.

Sikhism was founded by Nanak, the son of a corn merchant in Lahore. He may have been inspired by Kabir who tried earlier to reconcile the Moslem and Hindu religions. Nanak accepted a single God who provides spiritual liberation through prayer and deeds, but rejected image worship and denounced the Hindu caste system. According to the Reverend Charles Francis Potter, "Sikhism at its best was a blending of Bhakti Hinduism [loving devotion to a single God] with Moslem Sufism with its divine rapture of the God-possessed mystic."

Although he preached widely, Nanak inspired only a small number of followers in his native Punjab. These were drawn mainly from lower-caste Hindus who were glad to throw off the restraints of the caste system. Nanak was called the First Guru (teacher). His successor was given the title Second Guru. He and the Third Guru followed Nanak's original teachings, but the Fourth Guru, Ram Das, greatly expanded the religion. He was fortunate to live in the time of Akbar when religious tolerance was the national policy. He built a shrine which his successor, Granth, enlarged into the Golden Temple of Amritsar (Pool of Immortality).

Granth, who disliked the numbered guru titles of his predecessors, also compiled the *Adi Granth*, the Sikhs' Bible. He made the mistake, however, of aiding a rebellious son of Jahangir and was executed by the angry ruler in 1606. He was succeeded by his son, Hargovind. When his followers tried to put the royal robe of pearls about his neck, Hargovind refused, saying, "My necklace will be a sword belt!" He then turned the Sikhs from a peaceful group into a militant order, fanatically dedicated to fighting for their rights instead of meekly submitting to tyranny.

The Ninth Guru, Teg Bahadur, was the Sikh leader when Aurangzeb began his attacks on the Hindus and the heretical Moslems. Teg Bahadur resisted Moslem attempts to destroy Sikh temples. He was arrested by Aurangzeb and told to embrace the Moslem religion or be killed. He chose death and was decapitated in December, 1675. His successor was his son, Gobind, who became the Tenth Guru.

While Hargovind was the first to develop the Sikhs into a militant group, Gobind completed the work. Under his direction, the Sikhs become more of a fraternal lodge than a religion. (They have been compared to the Knight Templars of Europe's Middle Ages.) He called his creed *Khalsa*. Each member had to undergo initiation where he drank water stirred by a dagger, as part of the Baptism of the Sword, and then ate cakes made from consecrated flour. The members renounced caste and dietary restrictions. They were required to wear a distinctive dress and to keep on their persons at all times five objects whose names began with the letter K. These were *Kesh* (hair), *Kirpan* (sword), *Kachha* (short underwear), *Kanghi* (comb), and *Kara* (iron bangle). Gobind's intention was to fight fanaticism with fanaticism—and he succeeded.

In the meantime, Aurangzeb continued to slash his bloody way

through all of India. By 1690 he controlled the entire subcontinent from Bombay to Kabul in Afghanistan, and from the Himalaya Mountains in the north to Cape Comorin at the southern tip
of India. It was, however, an empire seething with revolt. His war-
weary subjects might have accepted Moslem rule if the emperor
had relaxed his religious fanaticism, but nothing could persuade
him from trying to destroy all opposition to orthodox Islam.

A history of the time recorded an anonymous letter sent to the
king. It pointed out that Akbar the Magnificent had treated all
religions as equal, but that Aurangzeb's policies had caused nothing but devastation and bloody reprisals. The letter read:

> If your Majesty places any faith in those books by distinc-
> tion called divine, you will be there instructed that God is the
> God of all mankind, not the God of the Moslems alone. Pagan
> and Moslems are alike in His Presence. Distinctions of color are
> His ordination. In your mosques, to His name the voice is raised
> in prayer. In a house of images [i.e., a Hindu Temple] when
> the bell is shaken, still He is the object of adoration. To vilify
> the religion or customs of other men is to set at naught the
> pleasure of the Almighty.

This passionate plea was ignored and the emperor continued to
the day of his death to fight all who opposed orthodox Islam. He
died in 1707 at the age of 89. Bahadur Shah, after fighting the
other sons of the dead emperor, became the new Mogul ruler.
Gobind Singh, the Sikh leader, had backed Bahadur, so the Sikhs
expected no opposition to their religion. Unfortunately, Gobind
was murdered by a Pathan in 1708. He had earlier abolished the
title of guru, as leader of the Sikhs, expressing the belief that the
religion's leadership should not be hereditary as it had been in
the past. Since he was the last of the direct bloodline of the founder,
Nanak, the title lapsed, and he is known to history as the "Last
Guru."

Leadership of the militant Sikhs passed to a military man,

named Banda. This man, known as the "False Guru," dressed as Gobind and passed himself off as the resurrected Gobind to arouse the Sikhs to fight a holy war with the Moslems. He then attacked the Moslem city of Sarhind, slaughtering the inhabitants and destroying the Mosques. Others among his followers attacked Lahore, but were driven back. However, they did gain control of the Punjab and Indian area between Lahore and the Mogul capital of Delhi. Bahadur Shah recaptured Sarhind and drove the Sikhs back into the hills from where they kept raiding Moslem settlements in North Punjab. After Bahadur Shah died, in 1712, the Sikhs came back from the hills to capture several important towns. The Moguls were too busy fighting three wars among themselves to fight the Sikhs. Finally, in 1715, Moslem troops from Lahore captured Banda and 740 of his fellow Sikhs. They were taken in chains to Delhi and executed. Banda was exhibited in an iron cage, and then was forced to witness the execution of his three-year-old son before he was beaten to death with clubs.

The Mogul Empire was slowly crumbling as ineffective rulers followed one after another. States conquered by Aurangzeb won their freedom and, once again, North Pakistan became a road for conquerors who sought the riches of India. In 1739, Nadir Shah—the Turk who had conquered Persia—invaded Afghanistan and captured Kabul from where he mounted a new invasion of Pakistan. He smashed the Mogul troops at Peshawar and, following the route of Alexander the Great, crossed the Indus at Attock. He captured Lahore by the end of the year, cut his bloody way through the Sikhs, and went on to sack Delhi. The invaders then retreated with their booty.

A new invasion came in 1748 when Ahmed Shah Abdali, an Afghan who became king of Kabul when Nadir Shah was assassinated, slashed a bloody path through North Pakistan. He sacked Lahore, but was defeated by the Moguls when he tried to move on to Delhi. The Punjab Sikhs suffered terribly during this invasion, for the Moslem Afghan delighted in slaughtering the heretic Sikhs. He destroyed the Sikhs' most sacred temple at Amritsar and defiled the ground by soaking it in cow's blood. The remaining Sikhs again fled to the hills.

After the invaders were defeated by the Delhi Moguls, the Sikhs came down from the hills and slaughtered every Moslem they could catch. The Moslems they killed were Punjabis who had also suffered at the hands of the invaders. This made no difference to the vengeful Sikhs: their victims were Moslems. Afterward, the Sikhs began to build a strong nation in the Punjab. Unfortunately for them, a thousand miles away, in East Bengal, a new enemy—the British East India Company—was on the horizon.

CHAPTER

7

British Conquest of India

In 1599, a group of London businessmen obtained a charter from Queen Elizabeth I, authorizing them to form a company to trade with the Orient. The resulting East India Company finally opened its first trading post in Bombay in 1614. British penetration of India was not to be challenged until the French settled in Madras in 1670. Later, the French would expand and directly challenge the East India Company's post in Bengal.

Although the royal charter authorized the East India Company to buy or seize and rule whatever land it could, the British considered it too expensive to rule an entire country. Now they were forced to set up an empire to keep it out of French hands. The French, determined to run the British out of Bengal, backed the

Nawab of Dacca, who controlled a large part of what is now Bangladesh.

In 1756, the Nawab attacked the British Fort William on the Hoogly River in what is now a section of Calcutta. A large number of British prisoners, taken in the battle, suffocated from being imprisoned in a small room. The story of the "Black Hole of Calcutta" so infuriated the British people that they backed Robert Clive, who defeated the Nawab in the Battle of Plassey in 1757. Clive then annexed the territory in the name of the East India Company. From this foothold the company began a systematic subjugation of the entire country. It took eighty years before they were in a position to threaten what is now West Pakistan.

The British policy was to destroy the Moslems' power while building up the Hindus. This was done to prevent the Moguls from trying to revolt. The Moslems now became second-class citizens in the land they had ruled for so long. This reverse discrimination served to keep open the breach between the two religions. If the directors of the East India Company had followed a policy of trying to reconcile the two, the ultimate division of India and Pakistan might not have been necessary. At this time, the East India Company operated like the government of a sovereign nation. The governor was literally King of India, answerable only to his "parliament," the company's Board of Directors in England. As time went by, the British government began to dominate the company's actions.

The area that is now Pakistan took advantage of the Mogul collapse to declare their independence. The Indus Valley was then divided into two independent states, the Punjab and Sind. The Sikh-controlled Punjab included all of northern Pakistan to the Khyber Pass on the Afghan border and south to a point below Multan on the Indus River. It was ruled by the famous Ranjit Singh. Sind extended from the southern frontier of the Punjab to the Arabian Sea. It was controlled by the Mirs Talpurs family who broke the area into numerous states ruled by members of the family.

By 1839, the East India Company controlled all of India up to the borders of the Punjab and Sind. The Sikhs in the Punjab, the Mirs in Sind and the Afghans across the mountains had nervously watched the British sweep across India. Now the conquering British were at their frontiers.

Ranjit Singh was the most remarkable of the rulers who faced the empire-hungry advance of the British. He was known to the Englishmen as "The Old Lion" from the suffix Singh (Lion) which all Sikhs attach to their single given names. (They do not have surnames.) Ranjit was born in 1780, the son of a ruler who controlled the original Punjab region between the five rivers. Ranjit became rajah when his father died, but the actual ruler was his mother who tried to dominate the twelve-year-old boy. She was a power-hungry tyrant, thoroughly hated by both her son and her people. The Rani—as she was called—was able to hold power because of her close association with the general of the army.

Ranjit chafed under her control. He wanted to be king in fact as well as in name. Youthful kings were no exception in feudal India. Babur had had full control of his kingdom at twelve and had led conquering armies when he was fourteen. Ranjit finally succeeded by murdering his mother when he was sixteen.

The young ruler faced a difficult political situation. While he was Rajah of the Punjab, he was actually a vassal of the King of Afghanistan. He was free to rule in the Punjab as long as he paid an annual tribute to the Afghan court. This went on until Afghan power began to weaken. Then Ranjit Singh went to war to increase his own power and territory. He succeeded in reaching Peshawar and the Khyber Pass. Earlier, he had driven the Afghans out of Kashmir.

Ranjit Singh was the kind of man about whom legends grow. He was wily, treacherous—and a magnificent warrior. He could outdrink any man of his time. His favorite drink—which only he had the constitution to stand—was made of raw corn alcohol mixed with opium and the blood of freshly killed meat. He loved parties, and it was said that his were the wildest orgies since the fall of Rome.

When Ranjit became king of Lahore, under the Afghans, he ruled a half million Sikhs who were renowned as warriors. Ranjit was smart enough to realize that they were warriors of the past who went galloping into battle like the invading Mongols of the Middle Ages, so he set out to modernize them. He first sent word to Europe that men who knew warfare could find good positions with him. At the same time, he sent his smartest young men across into India to enlist in the British forces. There were very few British troops in India. The East India Company used Indian troops under British officers to conquer the country. The Sikhs

An ancient fort, whose origin goes back to the days of Alexander the Great, was used by Ranjit Singh in his wars.

had orders to learn all they could and then desert, bringing back their newly gained military knowledge to the Punjab.

After the end of the Napoleonic wars in Europe, The Old Lion was able to secure the services of a number of veterans. In 1822, he hired two men, Jean Francois Allard and Jean Baptiste Ventura, who had walked from Europe across Persia and Afghanistan to join him. Both had been colonels in Napoleon's army. Ranjit Singh welcomed them, permitted them to take native wives and live like rajahs themselves, while they trained his troops in Napoleon's army tactics. The Old Lion realized that an army who had caused the British so much trouble was a good one to emulate in these troubled times when the British army was at his own frontier.

The undisciplined Sikhs resented their foreign teachers, hated the strict discipline of European tactics; as famous horsemen, they were furious at being forced into infantry battalions. But they feared and respected the Old Lion, so there was not even a hint of revolt during his lifetime. Although his army was so strong and well trained that even the British hesitated to attack him, Ranjit Singh did not like to risk his soldiers in actual battle. He blustered, threatened, and rattled his sword, doing all he could to frighten other princes into capitulating without a fight. But when forced to fight, he and his new army of Sikhs fought splendidly. In one of his battles with a prince of the collapsing Mogul empire, he captured the famous "Zam Zam" gun. This enormous cannon had originally been seized from the Afghans and then was used in a war between the Moguls and the Hindu Mahrattas. After Ranjit's death, it was used by the Sikhs against the British and, following the Sikh War, it was mounted on a pedestal in Lahore as a monument. Today, it is a famous tourist sight, known as "Kim's Gun," because the boyish hero of Rudyard Kipling's famous novel, *Kim*, played on it and called it "his gun."

Ranjit's iron constitution began to fail as he approached middle age. At fifty, he looked seventy-five. A stroke paralyzed one side of his body and left him incapable of talking. Still, he ruled. He grunted and waved his one good arm, while his sole remaining eye flashed fire. None dared to oppose him.

In 1838, the British became alarmed at Russian interest in Afghanistan and decided to march against the Afghans. They were well aware that Kabul, in Afghanistan, had been the traditional staging point for invasions of India since the days of the Aryans and Alexander the Great. It seemed prudent to secure this back-door to India before the Russians moved in. The British Governor General, Lord Auckland, asked and received permission from Ranjit Singh to march British troops across the Punjab for an attack on Afghanistan. The Old Lion had a double motive in granting this permission. He knew he would have to fight the British if he refused. But he also hated the Afghans, and he stood to win if their remaining power was smashed by the East India Company.

When the British army reached Ferozepore on the Sutlej River, the division between the Punjab and British India, Ranjit Singh held a *durbar*—official royal reception—for Lord Auckland. According to Donald Featherstone:

> Ranjit Singh had a magnificent tent standing in the middle of a magic garden aglow with rare shrubs and flowers. Brought in boxes from Lahore, they had transformed the arid area overnight. Everything was on a lavish scale—Ranjit's tent was of cashmere borne on solid silver poles and the furniture was inlaid with gold. His elephants were caparisoned in cloth-of-gold, their howdahs were inlaid with ivory, silver and ebony.

Ranjit was then so feeble he could not mount a horse. Instead, he rode out to meet his guests on an elephant while cannons boomed and trumpets shrilled a salute. His guard of honor was as splendidly caparisoned as the elephants, but the shrunken figure of the Old Lion outshone them all with the great Koh-i-noor diamond—"The Mountain of Light." (This most famous of all Indian diamonds was included in the booty of the Sikh War of

1845, after Ranjit Singh's death, and it is now part of the crown jewels of England.)

This glittering show of pomp and ceremony served as a send-off for the British on their way to Afghanistan. They captured Kabul in August, 1838, and placed their puppet, Shah Shuja, on the throne, intending to rule the country through him. When Ranjit Singh died soon afterward, a power struggle was launched that ended with the destruction of the empire that the Old Lion had created.

Eighteen months after Ranjit Singh's death, on June 30, 1839, the Afghans revolted against the British army of occupation. General Elphinstone, the commander, decided to evacuate his forces before they were slaughtered. He might as well have left them to die in Kabul, because vengeful hillmen from the Hindu Kush and Sulaiman Mountains ambushed them in the snow-choked passes. Some Punjabis wanted to attack the remnants of the British army who were retreating across North Pakistan on their way back to India, but the Sikhs were too badly divided to risk a war at this time. The struggle for power among the would-be successors of Ranjit Singh was rapidly destroying the strong army built up by the Old Lion.

The disastrous defeat in Afghanistan was a tremendous blow to British prestige. Much of the conquest of India had been accomplished because defending princes were convinced that the army of the East India Company was invincible, and that it was better to make a deal than be destroyed. It was company policy, whenever possible, to leave native princes in authority but subject to British control. Because these vassal princes could be expected to revolt, if it appeared that British military strength was slipping, something had to be done quickly to restore the awe and fear upon which the Indian authority of the East India Company had been based.

It must be remembered that at this time it was not the British Government, but the directors of the East India Company who ruled the Indian Empire. The army, although referred to as "British," was the private army of the company with British officers and, in many cases, noncommissioned officers. The bulk of the fighting troops were Indian. The British Government in London had lately begun to exert pressure through the company's court of directors. In earlier times, the company had been autonomous, but in later years no major action was taken without approval of the British prime minister. The company's solution to the loss of prestige, caused by the Afghan defeat, was to stage a conquest of Sind. Sind would provide a base for restaging a new invasion of Afghanistan as soon as conditions warranted.

In addition, the company was beginning to take an interest in Sind trade. A trading post had been established there, in the seventeenth century, but it had been unprofitable. Another attempt to trade with the desert kingdom was made in 1758, but it also had to be abandoned. Then, in 1827, a British surgeon sailed up the Indus to treat Mir Murad Ali who was ruler of Hyderabad, a city between Karachi and Multan. He was impressed by the commercial possibilities and wrote the company a glowing report. Irrigation, he said, would turn the Indus into another Nile, and the river was a natural trade route. He thought that trade goods, now carried by camels from the Khyber Pass across the Punjab into India, could be transported cheaper by boating it down the Indus to ships at Karachi. From there the ships would take the material to Bombay and southern Indian ports.

The difficulty was that the Indus flowed through a number of principalities, and each rajah extracted tolls and fees on all cargo. To eliminate this, British commercial agents forced unequal treaties on the rulers. These treaties were considered binding on the Mirs, but the East India Company kept revising them to increase the company's benefits. One of the Mirs, Mohammed Nur, complained: "Since the day that Sind has been connected with the British there has always been something new. Your government is never satisfied. We are anxious for your friendship, but we cannot be continually persecuted."

The British commercial agents argued that trade would increase Sind's wealth. Mohammed Nur replied bitterly, "You tell me my country will flourish. It is quite good enough for us, and not so likely to tempt the cupidity of its neighbors. Hindustan was rich, and that is the reason it is now under your subjugation."

Despite treaties forbidding the stationing of British troops in Sind, Lord Auckland seized Karachi and two other cities and used them as bases for the ill-fated attack on Afghanistan. He then loudly complained because the Mirs were slow in furnishing the baggage camels that the British had demanded. When the Mirs cited the treaties, Auckland retorted: "No treaty will be permitted to interfere with the needs of the paramount power on the continent." When the British lost the war in Afghanistan, the Mirs were tempted to attack the British in their countries, but they decided that they did not have sufficient strength. Also, they feared that, if the British did withdraw from Sind, their own states would be at the mercy of the Sikhs who had now become violently anti-Moslem. The Moslem Mirs knew they would be better off being robbed by the British than being slaughtered by the Sikhs.

The Afghan disaster caused Lord Auckland's recall, but his successor, Lord Ellenborough, was equally determined to annex Sind. He, too, envisioned the lower Indus Valley as another Egypt. He brought in Sir Charles Napier as commander-in-chief of British forces in Sind, and gave him complete authority to bring the native princes under control. Napier was also a veteran of the Napoleonic Wars and a very good soldier. He shared Ellenborough's enthusiasm for the future of Sind and began a systematic program to undermine the local princes by constantly accusing them of treachery and of plotting against the British. For evidence he had only an order from the King of Afghanistan to expel the British, reminding the Sind princes that they were his traditional vassals. When the princes took no action, a continual stream of forged letters, spy tales, and out-and-out lies provided excuses for Napier to invade the various provinces under the guise that they were plotting against him.

Napier's campaign against Mir Rustam, the most important of the Talpur Mirs, was especially aggressive. He constantly accused Rustam of treachery and, in December, 1842, the British invaded Rustam's principality when the Mir was slow to sign a new and more oppressive treaty. Napier's reply to a letter of protest from Rustam was: "I cannot go into arguments. I am only a commander for the Governor General. I will forward your letter to him, if you so desire me to do so, but in the meantime I will occupy the territories which he commanded me to occupy."

As Napier's ring of soldiers moved in closer, Rustam fled, but later he rallied an army of Sindhi and Baluchistan followers. Napier easily defeated Rustam and swept through the rest of Sind. The reaction in England was not exactly what Lord Ellenborough and Sir Charles Napier had expected. For some time, there had been increasing complaints in England about the highhanded activities of the East India Company and growing sympathy for the Indian princes whose kingdoms were overrun without real provocation. In the London *Morning Chronicle*, Sir Henry Pottinger stated that the treatment of the Mirs of Sind "was the most disgraceful and unprincipled that has ever stained our empire in India." Montstuart Elphinstone went farther. Referring to the growing belief in England that the Sind conquest was solely motivated by desire to rebuild British military prestige lost in the Afghan campaign, he said that the company's actions in Sind resembled those of a bully who had been knocked down in a street fight and then went home to beat his wife for revenge.

Sir Charles Napier received great credit for his military strategy in Sind, but Lord Ellenborough, as governor-general of India, was relieved and replaced by Sir Henry Hardinge in July, 1844. Hardinge was a veteran general of the Napoleonic Wars and a personal friend of the Duke of Wellington who had defeated Napoleon. Wellington, a former prime minister of England, was then Minister Without Portfolio in the cabinet of Sir Robert Peel. All these facts seemed to indicate that neither the East India Company nor the British cabinet had any intention of really slow-ing down the conquest of India. The fall of Sind only left the Punjab and the Northwest Territory still independent. The hill country of the Pathans was nominally under the Punjab, but the political situation in Lahore was so disturbed that the Punjab Government had little control over the tribes above and below Peshawar. The situation was ideal for conquest.

CHAPTER 8

Destruction of the sikhs

Sir Charles Napier expanded the irrigation systems while he was military governor. He also improved the port of Karachi, starting developments that eventually made Karachi the largest city in Pakistan. (Today, it has a population of more than a million and a half.)

While Napier was bringing an enforced peace to turbulent Sind, the Punjab lapsed into anarchy. Ranjit Singh's successor, his eldest son, Kharak Singh, was an imbecile who fell into the hands of unscrupulous advisers. This led to a palace revolution by Kharak's son, Prince Nau Nihal Singh. The prince was extremely popular and proved a good ruler, during the year he controlled the government in the name of his father. In 1840, however, while returning from the funeral of his father, Prince Nau Nihal was killed by an archway which collapsed as he rode under it.

Nau Nihal's successor, Sher Singh—who claimed to be a son of Ranjit Singh—lacked the strength to control the country. The army revolted, drove out its European advisers, dismissed many of its officers, and brought all government to a standstill for six months. The soldiers finally realized that the resulting anarchy left them open to British attack. Sher Singh then tried to reassert control, but was assassinated along with his prime minister, Dhian Singh. Dhian's son, Hira Singh, destroyed his father's murderers and seized control of the government. The new warlord was a brilliant young man. He knew that if he hoped to stay in power long enough to restore order, he would have to unify the Sikhs. He found what he sought in a five-year-old boy named Dulip Singh. The boy was the son of Ranjit Singh's widow, the Rani Jindan, who had been one of the Old Lion's four legal wives.

Ranjit Singh had been incapable of having any children during the last years of his life, but Hira's need to unify the people was so great that he accepted the Rani's claim that her child was the true blood of the Old Lion. He called on the country to unite behind this son of their greatest leader. The Sikhs accepted Dulip Singh, but they refused to accept Hira and he was slain in 1844. His place was taken by the Rani's brother who was executed by the army the following year. For the next six weeks, anarchy again reigned throughout the Punjab. This ended when the army was again convinced that the British were massing for an attack. There was considerable evidence that this might be so. When Lord Ellenborough left India, in 1844, there had been 17,612 British controlled troops along the Punjab border. Lord Hardinge, while openly claiming that there was no possibility of war between British India and the Punjab, increased the number of troops along the Punjab frontier to 40,423. Cannon was also increased from 66 big guns to 94. And his army commander-in-chief was Major General Hugh Gough, another veteran of the Napoleonic Wars.

Gough loved war. He was no headquarters soldier. In every battle, he put on a white "fighting coat," so that his troops could see him and join him in the forefront of the fighting. (This famous coat is preserved in a British war museum today.) He was a true soldier of the old school. Once when told that his guns had run out of ammunition, Gough, undismayed, said cheerfully, "Thank God for that! Now we can be at the enemy with our bayonets!"

With Gough and a doubled number of soldiers on their Indian frontier, and Sir Charles Napier with his victorious army on their Sind frontier, the Sikhs decided to get along among themselves while they dealt with the British threat. The Rani, as mother of the boy-rajah, Dulip Singh, was named regent. She then raised her lover, Lal Singh, to vizier and his friend, Tej Singh, to commander-in-chief of the army. The real power, however, continued to be held by the *Panchayets*—the army's council of five.

The rebellious army was eager to attack the British. Lal Singh and Tej Singh readily agreed to this, but with a sinister purpose in mind. They wanted the Sikh army to lose the war with the British, because this would destroy the army's power. They felt they would be better off ruling as British puppets than under the domination of the Sikh army, which they did not expect to survive for long. To insure that the British knew that they were secretly supporting the side of the East India Company, Lal Singh sent a messenger to General Littler who commanded British forces at Ferozepore on the British side of the Sutlej River frontier between the two countries.

So it happened that the Sikh army stormed across the Sutlej on December 11, 1845, with their commander-in-chief and prime minister secretly betraying them to the enemy. Both traitors, Lal Singh and Tej Singh, had been among the soldiers who massed just before the attack at the tomb of Ranjit Singh to vow fidelity in battle to the spirit of the Old Lion. General Sir John Littler's forces at Ferozepore were pitifully undermanned. Lal Singh knew this and, instead of attacking here as he should have, he ordered his army to bypass Ferozepore. The reason he gave was that it was senseless to waste time on the smaller garrison when they could strike the full British force instead.

Following this poor advice, the Sikhs charged ahead into British India. Sir Hugh Gough, accompanied by Governor-General Hardinge, came rushing with the main British army to meet the threat. On the 17th of December, the British straggled into Mudki, a Punjab village on the road to Ferozepore that had been abandoned by the Punjabis. The British made camp to rest after a fatiguing march. Supper was just starting when a messenger brought the news that the Sikhs were preparing an attack.

Gough hastily rallied his troops, charging out to meet the Sikhs who had gone into some sand hills covered with scrub bush. The battle became a melee that raged for two hours from sunset to twilight, until darkness made it impossible for the mixed-up forces to tell friend from foe. The Sikhs then withdrew toward Ferozepore, while the British went into bivouac. Since the British held the field, it was considered a victory, although Gough's forces suffered 872 killed and wounded. General Gough had shown poor judgement in attacking the Sikhs in the sand hills where the enemy held a tactical advantage.

Hardinge, as governor-general, was extremely dissatisfied with the showing made by the army. Many of the *Sepoys* (native troops) turned and ran; some even fired into the rear of their own troops ahead of them. Hardinge was technically the civil commander. Gough was commander-in-chief of the army, and held higher military rank than Hardinge. During the battle, when one of the field commanders was shot, Hardinge took over command of this officer's troops. Then, after the battle, Hardinge decided that he could not stand on his civilian status and miss the fighting. Despite his civilian rank of governor-general, he placed himself under Gough's command. Gough, flattered, immediately appointed Hardinge as his second in command.

The Sikhs pulled back to Ferozeshah, six miles from Ferozepore. General Gough ordered an immediate attack, but Hardinge used his authority as civil governor-general to countermand the commander-in-chief's order. Interference with a field commander in battle by a civilian authority was something unheard of in the British army. Nevertheless, Hardinge refused to permit the attack until General Littler brought up reinforcements from the by-passed garrison at Ferozepore. It was good that he insisted on the delay, for the battle of Ferozeshah on December 21st was one of the bloodiest of all the engagements fought by the British in India.

As at Mudki, the battle started in the late afternoon and extended into the night. Again, confusion reigned; even so, the fighting was heroic on both sides. The British had about 5,000 European troops and 12,000 Indians. They repeatedly stormed the Sikh emplacements in frontal attacks, only to be beaten back each time. The situation became so desperate that Governor-general Hardinge was sure that the battle was lost. Accordingly, he tried to save the thing he loved most—his sword. It had belonged to Napoleon and was given to Hardinge by the Duke of Wellington, after Waterloo, in 1816. Hardinge sent it to the rear by an aide. Although willing to die himself, rather than retreat, he could not let his precious relic be captured.

The British finally took the Sikh emplacements, but were driven back by a savage counterattack. The fighting then halted so that the exhausted soldiers on each side could get some rest. Later, Hardinge wrote to Sir Robert Peel:

> The night of the 21st was the most extraordinary of my life. I bivouacked with the men, without food or covering, and our nights are bitter cold. A burning camp in our front, our brave fellows lying down under a heavy cannonade, which continued during the whole night. . . . I remained until morning, taking very short intervals of rest. . . . My answer to every man was that we must fight it out, attack the enemy vigorously at daybreak, beat him, or die honorably in the field.

Both Hardinge and Gough were over sixty at the time, but each fought in the forefront of the bloody battle and shared every danger and inconvenience of the common soldiers. Gough's famous white "fighting coat" made him a splendid target, but by some miracle he was never hit, although his horse was shot from under him by cannon fire. The troops were without water and in the morning they licked the dew from their guns. This recalls Kipling's poem *Gunga Din* in which the famous chronicler of India said that in battle you do your work on water and "lick the bloomin' boots of him that's got it."

Gough and Hardinge, well aware that defeat now could unleash revolt throughout India and destroy the empire, mounted a desperate attack that drove back the bitterly fighting Sikhs across the Sutlej River. British casualties totaled 2,415. Sikh losses, first estimated by Gough as 5,000, were probably about the same.

Late in the afternoon of the 22nd, a fresh Sikh army appeared, personally led by Tej Singh. What happened, then, is still the subject of controversy. According to Jagmohan Mahajan's *Circumstances Leading to the Annexation of the Punjab* (a pro-Sikh, anti-British book published in Lahore):

> As the day advanced a second wing of the Sikh army commanded by Tej Singh appeared and the wearied and famished English saw before them a desperate and, perhaps, useless struggle. But this force mysteriously withdrew from the battlefield at a moment when the artillery ammunition of the English had failed, when a portion of their force was retiring from Ferozepore, and when no exertions would have saved the remainder if the Sikhs had boldly pressed forward. The Sikh cause was doomed with traitors in command.

Although some have tried to excuse Tej Singh's actions, it appears clear that he was determined to see the Sikh army destroyed in order to break the power it had over the government. He kept making a pretense of fighting, but used every excuse to avoid battle and to secretly inform the British command of Sikh plans, when he could not hold back his troops. In view of his and Lal Singh's conduct, the defense put up by the Sikhs at Ferozepore was nothing short of remarkable. Ferozepore was a victory for the British, but it was a hard one. Sir Henry Hardinge blamed

Gough for the high losses and secretly wrote to his friend, Prime Minister Robert Peel:

> Confidentially we have been in the greatest peril, and are likely hereafter to be in great peril, if these extensive operations are to be conducted by the Commander-in-Chief. Gough is a brave and fearless officer, an honorable and amiable man. . . . He deserves every credit for his heroism in the field . . . [but] he is not the officer who ought to be entrusted with the conduct of the war in the Punjab. . . . I respect and esteem Sir Hugh Gough, but I cannot risk the safety of India by concealing my opinion from you.

Hardinge asked that Sir Charles Napier be brought up from Sind to command the army of the Punjab. This letter was dispatched on December 30, 1845 but, due to the slowness of the mail, did not reach London until February 7th. An order, originating with the Duke of Wellington, was dispatched advising Hardinge to assume the duties of commander-in-chief in addition to governor-general. At the same time, the duke wrote a soothing, explanatory letter to Gough. Fortunately for Gough, the letters did not arrive until after the British had achieved two smashing victories, after an initial setback.

On January 21, 1846, the British took a severe beating, losing an important camel baggage train. Then, on January 28th, Sir Harry Smith smashed a Sikh attack at Aliwal and drove the Sikhs back across the Sutlej River. The Sikhs regrouped, and the decisive battle of the First Sikh War was fought at Sobraon, a mud-hut village on the British side of the Sutlej. Two days before the battle, Lal Singh secretly sent a messenger to the British with a map of the Sikh entrenchments to guide the attack by Gough. Later, the British, evidently conscience-stricken for having dealt with the traitor, claimed that "this information came too late to be of any other use than as confirming the intelligence we already had," as an official report put it.

At the height of the battle, the Sikhs began to retreat in order to regroup for a new attack. They had constructed a bridge of boats across the Sutlej to provide an avenue of escape, should the battle turn against them. But when they started across, they found that Tej Singh had sunk the center boat. According to Jagmohan Mahajan:

> Thrust back inch-by-inch, the Sikhs were hurled pell-mell into the river, into which they plunged, preferring death to surrender. Then followed a hateful scene of British butchery: "nearly ten thousand of the enemy were shot down by grape and shrapnel in the bed of the river which ran red with blood." (The statement in quotes is from J. B. Cunningham who wrote a history of the Sikhs in 1897.)

There have been bigger and bloodier battles in military history, but none have been fought with greater bravery on both sides. No one recognized this more than Sir Hugh Gough. While giving full credit to his own troops for their truly heroic charges, Gough did not neglect to praise a gallant enemy. In a letter to Sir Robert Peel, Gough wrote:

> Policy precludes me from publicly recording my sentiments on the splendid gallantry of our fallen foe, or to record the acts of heroism displayed, not only individually, but almost collectively by the Sikh officers and army; and I declare, were it not from a deep conviction that my country's good required the sacrifice, I could have wept to have witnessed the fearful slaughter of so devoted a body of men.

Sobraon destroyed the main Sikh Army. However, smaller Sikh armies were still intact at Peshawar and Amritsar. Hardinge decided that his battered forces lacked the strength to hold the Punjab. He was content to annex only that part on the east bank of the Sutlej River. He also took Kashmir, the magnificently beautiful region between the Punjab and the Himalaya Mountains. He knew that the British could not hold the rebellious Kashmir Valley against the vengeful Punjabi guerrillas who were sure to form. So he sold Kashmir to Gulab Singh, the rajah of Jammu, a small state bordering the Punjab and Kashmir. Gulab Singh had been sympathetic to the British. Hardinge then affirmed Dulip Singh as Maharaja of the Punjab and his mother, the Rani, as regent. The traitors Lal Singh and Tej Singh, retained their positions, but the resultant treaty made the Punjab a British dependency.

In London, the Duke of Wellington made a speech in Parliament in which he praised the British commanders at Mudki and Ferozeshah, but pointedly neglected to mention Sir Hugh Gough. When copies of the speech reached Lahore, in April, Gough was startled by the omission.

Then, on May 5, 1846, Sir Hugh received a letter which the duke had written in answer to Sir Henry Hardinge's request that Gough be relieved as commander-in-chief. The duke, after praising Gough, said delicately that the political situation in India demanded that the political head of the country, the governor-general, should also command the army. Gough flew into a rage. In a stiffly formal letter, Gough reminded Wellington that he had omitted Gough's name in his speech of thanks to the army. While speaking well of Hardinge, Gough said flatly he would not serve in a subordinate army position to a man who was his military junior. Accordingly, he tendered his resignation.

The war was over and Gough was a hero. Hardinge was well aware of the way the battered and wounded soldiers had cheered the old man, when he came down to the jammed field hospital to see them. He refused to accept Gough's resignation, and Gough remained commander-in-chief.

The British policy of trying to control North Pakistan through a puppet Punjab government got off to a bad start. The people of Kashmir took unkindly to being sold to the Sultan of Jammu. The British discovered that Lal Singh, their supposed friend, was inciting the Kashmiri to resist being taken from the Punjab and given to Gulab Singh of Jammu. Lal Singh was tried and exiled. The Sikhs, who hated their prime minister for his treacherously helping the British overrun the Punjab, were delighted by his ouster.

The exile of Lal Singh infuriated the Rani, for the deposed

prime minister had been the queen's lover. At first, she had welcomed the British to Lahore and begged Hardinge to leave troops in the capital to protect her from Sikh vengeance, but the exile of her lover made her realize that the British intended to rule. That meant her authority would vanish. The British resident to the Punjab would have the same total authority over the government that the governor-general of India exercised in Delhi. So the queen-regent began to conspire to bring the Sikh chiefs to her side for a future revolt against British domination.

Aware of the queen's agitation, Hardinge cancelled the provision of the Treaty of Lahore, ending the First Sikh War, which called for British troops to evacuate the Punjab by 1849. He sent a paper to the Sikh chiefs, stating:

> . . . if solicited to aid in the administration of the Government of the Punjab, during the minority of the Maharaja [the young Dulip Singh], the British agent must have full authority to interfere, and to control all matters, in every department of State, for the benefit of all concerned. . . . A British force will remain at Lahore for the protection of the city and country, in such position as the Governor-General should think best.

The Rani Jindan was deprived of all power, although, as mother of the ten-year-old Maharaja Dulip Singh, she still held the title of regent. Then, in February, 1847, Hardinge learned that the Rani was conspiring with some old retainers of the late Ranjit Singh to assassinate the British resident agent and Tej Singh, whom the queen blamed for her fall from power. Unfortunately for Hardinge, the evidence against the queen was so slight that he did not care to risk arousing Sikh sympathy for her by taking action. Thus, he decided to wait for a better chance.

That opportunity came shortly afterward, when the British planned to award those chiefs who had assisted them. These awards were to be presented by the ten-year-old Maharaja Dulip Singh at a colorful durbar. When Tej Singh came forward to receive elevation to a rajahship, the boy refused to mark the traitor's forehead with the saffron *teeka* of office. Henry Lawrence, the British resident, later wrote: "I thought it might be bashfulness, or a dislike to wet his finger in the saffron paste; but when I pressed the point in vain . . . His Highness folded his arms and shrunk back into his velvet chair, with a determination foreign to his age and gentle disposition."

Lawrence went on to give his opinion that the boy had been schooled by his mother to refuse any honor to Tej Singh. He urged that the Rani be banished from the Punjab, before she could cause any more trouble. Hardinge agreed, and Lawrence issued a proclamation in which he stated that "the Right Honorable the Governor-General of India, feeling the interest of a father in the education and guardianship" of the maharaja felt it absolutely "necessary to separate the Maharaja from the Maharani, his mother."

The banished queen wrote Lawrence a furious letter in which she said, "Surely royalty was never treated before in the way you are treating us! Instead of being secretly king of the country, why don't you declare yourself so? You talk of friendship and then put us in prison. Do me justice or I will appeal to London!"

But London was far away, and the cries for justice of a minor queen who opposed British will was a matter of small consequence.

CHAPTER 9

The British Raj

No one expected the Sikhs to submit to foreign domination any longer than necessary, so a second Sikh-Anglo war was just a matter of time. Hardinge was succeeded as governor-general in 1848 by Lord Dalhousie, a man in his mid-thirties who was ambitious both for himself and for his country. In a letter to a friend, Dalhousie wrote: "If not in my day, then assuredly in my successor's the curtain will fall on the Sikh dynasty. If it be not sponged out now, there will be no real tranquillity."

Dalhousie soon found an excuse to resume fighting the Sikhs. Mul Raj, the Sultan of Multan—the city on the Indus at the border of Punjab and Sind—revolted after a British tax change cut his revenues. He was soon joined by Sher Singh, a Sikh chief who had previously cooperated with the British. Dalhousie declared: "The task before me is the utter destruction and prostration of the Sikh power, the subversion of its dynasty, and the subjection of its people. This must be done promptly, fully and finally."

General Hugh Gough had been made a lord for his victories in the First Sikh War and was still commander-in-chief of East India Company forces in India. He was not eager to fight in the summer and wanted to put off reconquest of the Punjab until fall. However, uprisings at the Northwest Frontier forced the British to evacuate Peshawar in the Khyber Pass region.

Dalhousie wrote to his lieutenant governor in the Punjab: "The rebellion of Sher Singh . . . and the state of the Sikh population everywhere, have brought matters to that crisis I have for months been looking for: and we are now, not on the eve of but in the midst of war with the Sikh nation and the Kingdom of the Punjab."

Though older, Lord Gough had not changed. He was still the same audacious, personally brave and stubborn commander that he had always been. Some of his enemies claimed that he wasn't brave at all, but was just too stupid to understand that he might possibly be killed. His military tactics had not changed either, and his idea of war was to meet the enemy head-on and slug it out. As a result, he suffered a defeat at Ramnagar on November 22nd, and nearly lost another in December. Dalhousie sent Gough an order to be more careful, and Gough stopped to wait for reinforcements. But in January he received word that Attock on the Indus, near Peshawar, had also fallen to the rebels. This forced Gough to attack to keep the rebels in Attock from joining up with the main Punjabi army in the Lahore area.

Gough met the Sikhs at the village of Chilianwala, near the Jhelum River. It was almost a repetition of the Battle of Ferozeshah. Once again, Gough insisted on attacking in the late afternoon. It was said that he had intended to wait for morning, but had become infuriated when the Punjabis shot at him while he was making an inspection. The British had to fight through thorny bushes to overrun the Sikh emplacement, but won at a bloody cost. When word reached London that Gough had 2,338 casualties in the fighting, there was a demand for his recall before his victories killed every man in the British army.

Earlier, the aged Duke of Wellington had asked Sir Charles Napier to take command in India. Napier, who was in bad health, declined. Now the duke wrote, "If you do not go, I must go myself." Napier reluctantly accepted. But as happened in the First Sikh War, Gough pulled off another decisive victory before his replacement could arrive. The battle took place at Gujrat on February 21, 1849. This defeat ended Sikh resistance. Later, many Sikhs enlisted for service in the British army where they served with outstanding fidelity.

On March 29, 1849, Lord Dalhousie called a *durbar* (court reception) in Lahore. Here, in a magnificent display of pomp, his representative, Henry Elliott, read a proclamation: "Wherefore the Governor-General of India has declared and hereby proclaims that the kingdom of the Punjab is at an end; and that all the territories of Maharaja Dulip Singh are now and henceforth a portion of the British Empire in India." Dalhousie also charged the Sikhs a heavy indemnity and forced the government to give the famous Koh-i-noor diamond to the British collection of crown jewels. Some Sikhs protested that Dalhousie should not force the abdication of Dulip Singh, since the maharaja was a minor and certainly not responsible for the revolt against the British. Dalhousie replied coldly, "I must dissent entirely from the soundness of this doctrine."

The Sikh nation was ended. British *raj* (rule) extended from the Afghanistan border in the west to the Bay of Bengal in the east, and from the Himalaya Mountains in the north to Cape Comorin at the tip of the continent.

In 1857, the *sepoys* (native troops) in Bengal revolted and the "Indian Mutiny" spread with alarming speed across India. The eastern sector of the Indian state of Bengal—across the subcontinent from Pakistan—was then, as now, predominantly Moslem.

The people were basically of Hindu origin, but had eagerly accepted the Moslem religion to escape the rigid Indian caste system. They were despised by the Hindus both as heretics and for their low-caste origin. Under the former Moslem-Mogul government, which naturally favored those of the Moslem faith over Hindus, the Moslem Bengalis had developed a landed gentry. Then, after Robert Clive's victory over the Moguls at Plassy, in 1757, the Moslems fell on lean years because the British favored the Hindus in order to keep the Moslem Moguls from regaining their lost power. As a consequence, the Moslems were seeking some way to break the British power and restore Mogul supremacy.

While a number of reasons have been given for the Mutiny of 1857, it seems clear today that the conspiracy was actually plotted by a few Moslem princes in Bengal. It spread quickly, involving uprisings, both by Moslem and Hindu groups throughout all India, except Pakistan. The Sikhs of the Punjab remained loyal to the British and kept the revolt from spreading into the area that now comprises the nation of Pakistan. The revolt failed simply because the Moslem and Hindu rebels could not work together. Although the rebels captured Delhi, at one point, the revolt was crushed within a year.

The mutiny jolted the British cabinet and brought about the end of the East India Company. The cabinet, working through a secretary of state for India, assumed responsibility for governing the Indian empire. A viceroy of British India replaced the East India Company's governor-general. Since the British blamed the Moslems for the mutiny, the Hindus were favored over Moslems for all government positions. Except for some of the tough Pathans of the Northwest Frontier Province (centering around Peshawar and the Hill Country), the British army in India shunned the Moslems. They concentrated on enlisting Sikhs who hated the Moslems with a ferocity more suited to the Middle Ages than to modern times.

The Moslem communities in India found themselves shut off

from jobs in government, education, and business. English law, which often conflicted with Moslem law and tradition, was forced upon reluctant Moslems. In Moslem eyes, this comprised a combined Hindu-Christian attack upon Islam. The British policy thus contributed to increased religious hatred between Moslems and Hindus at a time when every effort should have been made to find some common ground for unity of the Indian people.

The growth of Indian nationalism, spurred by the Hindus, brought about a change in British attitude. In 1885, the National Indian Congress was formed in Bombay. Its original purpose was to push for social reform, but it soon changed into a Hindu-dominated drive for independence from Great Britain. As Indian nationalism increased, the British took some steps to cultivate Moslem good will. In 1905, the government divided the province of Bengal to separate the predominantly Moslem east section from the Hindu west portion. This move was hailed by the Moslems, but furiously denounced by the Hindus. Finally, under Hindu pressure, the division was canceled in 1911; however, while it lasted, the province of East Bengal approximated the future East Pakistan which became Bangladesh in 1971.

The increasing demand for Indian self-rule alarmed the Moslems. Sir Sayyid Ahmed Khan, a noted Moslem leader, stated:

> If the English should leave India, then who would be the country's rulers? Our two nations, the Mohammedan and Hindu, could not sit on the same throne and be equal in power. It is necessary that one of them should conquer the other and thrust it down. To hope that both could remain equal is to desire the impossible and the inconceivable.

Both sides had seen their religions attacked by the other and feared that it would happen again. With this fear predominant, the events of the last part of the nineteenth century and the first forty-seven years of the twentieth century were dominated by religious politics. Some very farsighted men attempted to bring the two religious groups together for the good of India and themselves, but this proved impossible. The very foundation of Islam is that it is the only *true* religion, and all who do not profess it are heretics. Each Moslem has a mandate from heaven to fight a *jihad*—holy war—against the unbelievers. With such an attitude on the part of the Moslems, cooperation would have been impossible, even if the Hindus had been willing to make concessions—which they were not. The stage was being set for the bloody showdown that marked the end of British Raj and the painful ripping apart of India which created Pakistan and then Bangladesh.

Two remarkable men stand out in the turbulent years that led to India's independence and the formation of Pakistan as an independent nation. These men were Mohammed Ali Jinnah (*Quaid-i-Azam*, the Great Leader), and Mohandas K. Gandhi (the *Mahatma*, Great Soul). Jinnah led the Moslem faction and became the father of Pakistan. Gandhi was the catalyst behind Indian *Swaraj*—self-rule. Their political difference can be summed up in Jinnah's insistence upon the formation of a separate Moslem India and Gandhi's cry, "If you cut India in two, you must first cut me in two also."

Jinnah was tall and so thin that, except for his haughty face, he looked like an artist's conception of Don Quixote. Until his last years, he dressed in the most elegant English fashion and affected a monocle which he handled—so one acquaintance said—with the flair of an actor. He had a cold personality, disliked crowds, and was totally unable to compromise on anything. Yet, despite these handicaps, Jinnah welded the Indian Moslems into a solid force that withstood the pressure of both the British and the Hindu forces of Gandhi and Pandit Nehru.

The records say that Mohammed Ali Jinnah was born in October, 1875, but Jinnah said it was on Christmas Day, 1876. His family may not have been as wealthy as later writers claimed, but they were well-to-do in relation to the times. He received the best education available to a native boy in India and was married at fifteen to a fourteen-year-old girl, in accordance with the customs of the times. The next year, he was sent to England to be trained as a lawyer. His wife died during the second year he was in London.

When he was 23, and still studying in England, Jinnah got his baptism in politics. Dadabhai Naoroji, a Parsi Indian from Bombay, ran for a seat in Parliament in the elections of 1892. Jinnah vigorously electioneered for his fellow-Indian, after a prominent British politician contemptuously said that he never thought he would live to see the day when the British electorate could send a "man of color" to Parliament. Naoroji was elected by a mere majority of three votes, but this was sufficient to convince Jinnah of the fairness of the constitutional system—a conviction which remained with Jinnah for the rest of his life. In time, it would have a profound influence on Moslem-Hindu cooperation, for it caused Jinnah to reject the civil disobedience policies of Mohatma Ghandi, and this widened the rift between Hindu and Moslem in India.

Jinnah returned to India in 1897, but practiced law in Bombay rather than in his native city of Karachi. He was the only Indian lawyer in the huge commercial city, and Indians felt they could trust him more than they could trust English lawyers. Although his arrogance grew to the point where it was almost insufferable, his practice continued to grow and he became very wealthy. In a time when young bachelors were noted for their wild parties, Jinnah lived with a beloved sister in a very opulent house in Bombay. The only talk, approaching scandal, ever attached to his name, was whispers that he ate pork and drank English whiskey —both abominations in the eyes of true followers of Islam.

During the first nine years, after his return to India, Jinnah took no interest in politics. But, in 1906, Dadabhai Naoroji, whom Jinnah had helped elect to Parliament during his student days, persuaded the young lawyer to join the Indian National Congress. He became quite prominent in the organization and joined the All-India Moslem League in 1913. The league had been formed in 1906 by the Aga Khan, spiritual leader of the Ismaili sect of Islam, Mohammed Iqbal, and others. He also joined the Home

Rule League of Mrs. Annie Besant. Jinnah's avowed purpose at the time was to bring the Moslem League and the Hindu-dominated Indian National Congress closer together.

Jinnah's influence in the Indian National Congress suffered a setback, after the arrival of Mohandas K. Gandhi in 1915. Gandhi, like Jinnah, was an Indian of a wealthy family who had trained for the law in England. But, unable to prosper as a lawyer in his native country, Gandhi had gone to South Africa where he lived, prospered, and became involved in politics in order to aid the plight of Indians in the British colony.

From the first, the two detested each other, although Gandhi—mindful of the need for Moslem support in the struggle to oust the British from India—tried to cultivate Jinnah.

Toward this end, Gandhi got the National Congress to support the Moslem Califate (*Khilafat*) movement. This movement envisioned a united Moslem spiritual union that centered around the Caliph of Turkey, the titular head of the Islamic religion. This support appealed to the Moslems and many joined the Indian National Congress because of it. Then the Califate movement collapsed, after Kemal Ataturk seized power in Turkey in 1924 and abolished it.

In the meantime, Jinnah was growing increasingly dissatisfied with the way Gandhi and his disciple, Jawaharlal Nehru, were dominating the Indian National Congress. After the collapse of the Califate movment, he withdrew from the Congress and, in 1928, left India for England. His intention was never to return.

Being a proud, arrogant man, who never discussed his motives, Jinnah's real reason for deserting India is open to speculation. Some have claimed it was due to jealousy of Gandhi and Nehru. These people like to quote Louis Fischer, an American journalist, to whom Jinnah said in an interview: "Nehru worked under me in the Home Rule Society. Gandhi worked under me." Jinnah went on to say that he worked for Hindu-Moslem unity "until 1920 when Gandhi came into the limelight. A deterioration of Hindu-Moslem relations set in."

Others have claimed that his self-removal from India was

caused by despair over the bloodshed and riots between Hindus and Moslems. The worst of these disorders was in Calcutta in 1926. It started when a Hindu procession played loud music as they passed a Moslem mosque during prayer. The riot quickly spread over the city and several hundred people were slaughtered, Hindu and Moslem stores looted and burned, and temples and mosques desecrated. (Fighting between men of the two warring religions had begun on a lesser scale in 1923 and would continue until 1927.)

After Jinnah's departure the Moslem League's fortunes dropped, while those of Gandhi's Indian National Congress grew stronger. It became clear that Great Britain could not hold on to India for many more years. This situation increased Moslem fears of what would happen to them under total Hindu rule. League leaders realized that they lacked a leader who could unify the various Moslem factions. The League had never been a mass movement. Its activities were confined mainly to upper-class Moslems. Jinnah had been the only man with the strength of character to provide this leadership. Aga Khan III, the Ismaili leader, had been League president until 1914; but now, he was more interested in his English race horses, his villa on the Riviera, and his French wife, than in politics.

A delegation approached Jinnah in 1934, but he was reluctant to return. He was still embittered toward Gandhi and Nehru, especially at the way Gandhi was deliberately injecting the Hindu religion into politics. Finally, he agreed to return to India to do what he could. Curiously, this man, who would lead the fanatically religious Moslems, was himself a nonreligious man. His family was of the Khoja sect of Hinduism, and Jinnah himself accepted conversion to Islam in the late 1920's in order to marry the 18-year-old daughter of a Parsi merchant in Bombay.

This second marriage to a teenage girl, when he was in his late forties, was a tragedy for Jinnah. It was said that she was as beautiful as a blooming rose, fun-loving, and thoroughly spoiled by her doting family. The marriage was marked by separations and reconciliations until, during their last separation, Mrs. Jinnah became ill and died. Jinnah, proud and aloof, kept his thoughts about his wife to himself. Shortly before his death, in 1948, an acquaintance published a biography of Jinnah. It contained a picture of the late Mrs. Jinnah and a brief account of the marriage. The second edition of the book omitted the picture, although it was still listed in the photographic credits. A note had been added that the picture had been removed at the request of Jinnah. He also requested that mention be added that he had not, as rumor claimed, received a large marriage dowry from his wife's rich family. On the contrary, he claimed, he had taken nothing. However, Jinnah let stand the references to his dead wife in the text. He never married again, but lived with Fatima Jinnah, his devoted sister.

Among those who come to London, especially to implore Jinnah to return, was a Moslem aristocrat named Liaquat Ali Khan. Jinnah immediately liked the ardent young Moslem and he also admired Liaquat's young bride. More than just beautiful, the Begum Liquat Ali Khan was as politically minded as her husband. Indeed, today she is governor of the Pakistan province of Sind.

Jinnah listened to Liaquat's pleadings and asked, "But what would I return to in India? Does the League have a program—an ideal—a direction?" In the end, Liaquat had to return to India and report that he had failed to move Jinnah. The next year, 1935, Great Britain tried to dampen the growing clamor for Indian independence by passing an act permitting Indian government officials to be elected in the provinces. Before them, they had been British appointees. Jinnah decided that the provincial elections provided an opportunity for Moslem unity to make inroads into the popularity of Gandhi's Indian National Congress.

He returned to India and was elected president of the Moslem League. Liaquat Ali Khan became as close to Jinnah as Nehru was to Gandhi. The two electioneered hard, but the result was a disaster. In heavily Moslem Bengal, the League won only 37 out of a possible 119 seats. This was practically a landslide compared to the Punjab where only one delegate to the 86-seat assembly was elected. In the Northwest Frontier Province (centering around the famed Khyber Pass), the League failed to win a single seat.

A jubilant Nehru infuriated Jinnah with the statement that this proved that there were only two political parties in India: the British and the Indian National Congress. Mohammed Iqbal, nearly blind and slowly dying, wrote Jinnah a letter. The old poet pointed out that the League had lost the election because it was essentially a rich man's party. "The League will have to finally decide," he wrote, "whether it will remain a body representing the upper classes of Indian Moslems or the Moslem masses who have so far, with excellent reason, taken no interest in it." Iqbal added that the economic plight of the Moslem community was growing worse, and that this was due to a stranglehold on the Moslem farmers by Hindu moneylenders.

Jinnah was not yet in sympathy with the idea of Pakistan. He still believed that Moslem and Hindu unity could be achieved, and he therefore took no interest in Iqbal's suggestion. Iqbal died in 1938, mourned by the nation, but not by Jinnah.

When World War II began in Europe, in 1939, it proved to be a blessing for the Moslem League. The Indian National Congress, following the lead of Gandhi and Nehru, began a campaign of civil disobedience against the British who were sorely tried in their fight for existence against Hitler in Europe. Gandhi and Nehru were jailed several times, during the course of the war. Jinnah and the Moslem League fully supported the British. As a result, the league grew in strength and power. By 1940, Jinnah had come to realize that he could never make peace with Gandhi and Nehru.

So, at the 1940 Moslem League's annual convention in Lahore, Jinnah permitted a resolution to be introduced that called for an "autonomous and sovereign" nation of Indian Moslems. At the same time, Jinnah realized that Iqbal had been right: he could

achieve nothing unless he worked for the betterment of the Moslem masses, instead of concentrating upon the elite. Jinnah began
to remake the Moslem League toward this end, dominating it like
a dictator. Now, for the first time in his life, he achieved popular
acclaim. He had always been popular with his fellow-Moslem
politicians, but now crowds cheered him. He became *"Quaid-i-
Azam"*—The Great Leader—a title he carried to the day of his
death.

The war, ending in 1945, left Great Britain exhausted. Jinnah
was in a stronger position than he had ever been, and all of India
was in a turmoil. Gandhi and Nehru were demanding immediate
independence. Winston Churchill observed sourly that he had not
become prime minister to preside over the liquidation of the British empire. But Churchill lost the next election, and his successor,
Clement Atlee, realized that nothing short of a full-scale war
could hold India. He sent Sir Stafford Cripps to India with a plan
for an interim government, as a prelude to complete self-rule
(*swaraj*).

Jinnah violently denounced this plan as subordination of the
Moslems to the Hindus. When he refused to permit his league
members to join the interim government, the British decided to
go ahead and implement the plan without Moslem membership.
Jinnah immediately called for a "Direct Action Day" in protest.
When the National Congress also called for its members to dem-
onstrate on the same day (August 16, 1946), the stage was set for
bloodshed and tragedy.

The first explosion came in Calcutta. When Hindus tried to
stop Moslems from marching to a demonstration, in front of the
provincial government building, the battle began. It ended with
5,000 people killed and 20,000 more injured. Hundreds of homes,
stores, and public buildings were looted and burned, as the
screaming, vengeful mob vented their religious hatred.

In Calcutta, the Hindus took the worst of the battle, but in
Bihar, where another riot broke out, the Moslems were the major
sufferers. Newspaper accounts of rioting are often exaggerated,

A bronze statue of Mahatma Gandhi in Calcutta where vicious race riots occurred between the Hindus and the Moslems.

but in the Bihar tragedy we have the eyewitness account of General Sir Francis Tuker, who wrote in his memoirs, *While Memory Serves*:

> . . . practically every Moslem man, woman and child was murdered with appalling cruelty. Either here or later even pregnant women were ripped up, their unborn babies torn out and the infants' brains bashed out on walls and on the ground. . . . Women and children were seized by the legs by burly fiends and torn apart. These hellions looted and burned, casting the dead and dying into the flames.

There was a slight respite, and then the terror shifted from Bengal and East India to the Punjab. Atlee, in London, frightened by the ferocity in India, replaced Lord Wavell as Viceroy of India, and appointed Lord Louis Montbatten, the World War II hero who had organized the famed British Commandos. At the same time, he announced on February 20, 1947, that the British would turn over sovereignty to India in June, 1948.

This was the spark that set fire to the Punjab. The Sikhs were a minority, outnumbered by the Moslems and Hindus. Under the agreement to which Jinnah, Gandhi, and Nehru had finally agreed, Pakistan would be made up of provinces that had a pre-dominantly Moslem population. This would put the Punjab into Pakistan and Bengal into India. East Bengal had a predominant Moslem population, but Bengal as a whole had more Hindus. The furious Sikhs cried that they would kill every Moslem in India before they would be ruled. Then Montbatten, after a hurried trip to London, announced that the British pullout had been moved up to August 15, 1947.

The Sikhs and Moslems in Punjab had been murdering each other and burning villages since the previous March. The trouble in the Punjab and in Bengal convinced Jinnah, Nehru, Gandhi, and Montbatten that both Bengal and the Punjab would have to be divided.

Cutting two states—Bengal and the Punjab—in half posed tremendous problems, but none of those planning the partition dreamed that the reaction would be as bad as it turned out. Some writers have claimed that not since the invasion of Genghis Khan was there so much bloodshed and destruction in India.

The drawing of the actual partition line in the Punjab was entrusted to the Radcliffe Commission, headed by a distinguished British lawyer, Sir Cyril Radcliffe. It was an impossible job. In the end, the commission, doing the best it could, split the prov-ince along the line of the majority population. The anguished Sikhs lost the larger part of the great irrigation system they had paid for, as well as their historic city of Lahore.

During the previous Sikh-Moslem uprisings, Nehru visited one of the riot areas in East Punjab. Afterward, he observed: "I have seen ghastly sights and have heard of behaviors which would degrade brutes. If politics are to be conducted in this way, then they cease to be politics and become some kind of jungle warfare."

The new wave of terror, bloodshed and destruction, following the announcement of the partition line, made the earlier riots seem very tame indeed.

CHAPTER

10

The Tragedy of Partition

"The Sikhs saw that the boundary award was worse even than they had feared. Their lands, their canals, their homes in the rich and fertile West fell within the boundary of Pakistan. They became mad with rage," wrote S. K. Majumdar in his account of the terrible days that immediately followed the partition of Punjab.

The award was announced on the morning of August 17, 1947, and by that evening Gandhi, in Calcutta, received a wire from a Hindu follower in the Punjab. He reported that "a terrible massacre of Hindus is in progress in Lahore. The carnage surpasses Rawalpindi [site of an earlier riot]. Hundreds of dead are lying strewn on the roads. The greater part of the city is in flames."

Neither Gandhi, nor anyone else, could stop the inflamed Sikhs.

They refused to live in West Punjab under Moslem rule and were determined that no Moslems would remain alive in East Punjab under their own control. Panic-stricken refugees—both Sikhs and Moslems—began to flee from each other's territory. The London *Times* reported from the Punjab: "The Sikhs are clearing East Punjab of Moslems, butchering hundreds daily, forcing thousands to flee westward, burning Moslem villages and homesteads, even in their frenzy burning their own."

The slaughter stopped only when there were no more Moslems to kill. Meanwhile, the retaliatory slaughter of Sikhs and Hindus went on in West Punjab. British writer, Leonard Mosley, in his book *The Last Days of the British Raj*, stated: "Communal frenzy gripped the people on both sides of the border [the partition line] taking a heavy toll of lives and creating an exodus of population between the two dominions, the like of which has never been known before."

Sir Francis Tuker gave this account of the sickening events in Amritsar: "The Sikh gangs began to concentrate their attention on those who could not hit back and resorted to the murder of unarmed citizens, to rape, abduction and arson. Throughout, the killing was premedieval in its ferocity. . . . The Sikhs cried 'Rawalpindi!' as they struck home." The battlecry revived memories of Sikhs who had been slaughtered by the Moslems in earlier riots. In another portion of his book, Sir Francis told how the day of partition was "strangely celebrated in the Punjab. During the afternoon, a Sikh mob paraded a number of naked Moslem women through the streets of Amritsar, raped them and then hacked some of them to pieces with *kirpans* [the Sikh religious saber] and burned the others alive."

Bengal, too, was also split into an eastern and western state. There was some disorder, with Hindus fleeing from Moslem's East Bengal, which became East Pakistan, but it was minor compared with the carnage in West Pakistan. The Moslem Bengalis had never been as strong for partition as the West Pakistanis.

When Lord Montbatten turned over British *raj* (rule) to

Nehru, as prime minister of independent India, and to Jinnah, as governor-general of the newly created Pakistan, India was more prepared for *swaraj* (self-rule) than Pakistan. The Moslem League sorely was in need of leadership above and beyond Jinnah himself. For more than ten years, Jinnah had been a complete dictator of the Moslem League, determining all its policies. Now, with the sudden arrival of independence, the entire burden of building a national government from nothing fell upon the ailing shoulders of Quaid-i-Azam, the Great Leader.

In those first trying days, Jinnah proved his right to the title. There were no elections. He appointed himself governor-general, and no one challenged him. He made Liaquat Ali Khan, his long-time associate, prime minister, and together they set up a capital

Partition brought worsened conditions to East Pakistan, already plagued by extreme poverty and substandard living conditions like this slum area in Dacca, the provincial capital.

in an office building in Karachi. He asked British administrators to remain as governors of the various provinces. Although he tried to cope with his enormous problems, his government was impoverished. His country was flooded with refugees who had poured into West Pakistan to escape the terror in India. The national economy was stagnant, and the farmers—who made up the bulk of the population—were little more than serfs to absentee landlords. Rich Moslem merchants from Bombay, Delhi, and other Indian cities, flocked into West Pakistan. Some were refugees from Hindu retaliation, but others saw an opportunity for increased wealth and wanted to take over the economy of the new nation.

In East Pakistan, conditions worsened. India, hating the partition from the first, hoped to force Pakistan's return through economic pressure. This measure hit East Pakistan the hardest. West Pakistan was the largest sector of the nation in size, but East Pakistan, with its 47,000,000 people, compared to the west portion's 33,000,000, was largest in population. In 1947 all of East Pakistan's foreign exchange depended upon the export of tea and jute, the fiber from which gunny sacks are made. Tea and jute from East Pakistan also furnished 70 per cent of the entire Pakistani foreign exchange.

The vital jute industry was shut down by the partition. The growers were in East Pakistan, but the factories that processed the fiber were in India's Calcutta, over in West Bengal. India cut off importation of jute fiber, adding to the already devastating economic distress in East Pakistan.

At the same time, Jinnah was faced with the threat of war with India over the State of Jammu and Kashmir, one of the three princely states that the British had left for political reasons outside the regular Indian government. In the past, they had been ruled by their hereditary rajah monarchs. Under the terms of the partition, the people of these states (Jammu and Kashmir, Junagadh, and Hyderabad) were to decide by free election whether they wished to join one of the two new nations or remain independent. In 1948, India invaded Hyderabad when the *Nizam* (ruler) advocated independence. There were no complaints from foreign countries or in the newly formed United Nations over this definite aggression on the part of India.

Junagadh was an entirely different problem from Kashmir. Junagadh, a state ruled by a Moslem rajah, had a predominantly Hindu population. The situation was reversed in Kashmir. There the people were mostly Moslem, but their ruler was Hindu. The Moslem rajah of Junagadh declared for Pakistan without consulting his Hindu subjects. Jinnah made a grievous tactical error in immediately accepting the rajah's offer to join Pakistan. In so doing, he gave unspoken sanction to the promise that a ruler of a princely state had the authority to make such a decision without a popular vote, as called for by the partition agreement. India refused to accept the decision and overran the state.

In Jammu and Kashmir—generally just called Kashmir by foreigners—the Hindu prince wanted to retain his independence. But revolts in Jammu, and an invasion by Pathans from Pakistan's Northwest Frontier state, frightened him. As the invaders moved in on Srinagar, the capital in the exceptionally beautiful Vale of Kashmir, the maharaja fled. He begged India for aid, but Nehru —himself a native of Kashmir—refused to help, unless the prince ceded Jammu and Kashmir to India. This he did with great reluctance. Immediately, India dispatched Sikh soldiers into Kashmir. They drove back the Pathans and saved the Vale of Kashmir from capture.

Jinnah was on the verge of sending Pakistani troops to aid the so-called Pathan volunteers, but the Pakistani army was still officered by British army men. The British commander told Jinnah that Lord Montbatten called the Indian invasion of Kashmir perfectly legal. If Jinnah sent the army into Kashmir, then all British officers would have to resign, and Jinnah had no trained Pakistanis to take their place. He had to content himself with secretly helping the Pathan invaders as best he could.

General Sir Claude Auchinleck, who was still serving as commander of the Indian army until a general staff could be trained, reported to London: "I have no hesitation whatever in affirming that the present India Cabinet are inplacably determined to do all in their power to prevent the establishment of the Dominion of Pakistan on a firm basis." He might well have added that neither Montbatten nor any of the major British army officers wanted Pakistan to succeed. For some peculiar reason of parochial pride, they wanted to hold intact the entire empire that England had built in India—even though it no longer belonged to them.

The fighting continued in Kashmir, and the touchy political problem became one of the first international controversies to confront the newly formed United Nations. Nehru, in a statement made soon after the Kashmir fighting started, said that India favored an election to determine the will of the Kashmiri people. This did not please Jinnah. Despite its Moslem majority, the people of Kashmir were also ardent followers of Sheikh Mohammed Abdullah, the "Lion of Kashmir." Abdullah hated Jinnah and tended to favor India, even though he was a confirmed Moslem himself.

Jinnah did not want an election in Kashmir until he could undermine Abdullah's influence. However, Jinnah did not live to see the outcome. Worn out by overwork, he collapsed during a trip to North Pakistan. He was flown back to Karachi where he died on September 11, 1948. Jinnah had been supreme as governor-general, but his successor, Khwaja Nizamuddin, was a mere figurehead. The real power was held by Prime Minister Liaquat Ali Khan (Jinnah's long-time associate), a man who lacked Jinnah's popular appeal.

India's leaders exulted. They were certain that the dead Quaid-i-Azam Ali Jinnah had been all that held Pakistan together. They hoped that his death would cause the country to collapse. Then it would be reabsorbed into India. Foreign diplomats also thought this very likely.

Meanwhile, in Kashmir, India held Poonch, Jammu, and most of the Vale of Kashmir. The Azad Kashmiri rebels held the north-

Mohammed Ali Jinnah, who died Sept. 11, 1948, is buried in a magnificent mausoleum in Karachi. The tomb shown here, in a room open to the public, is a replica of the true tomb under the mausoleum which is never open to public view.

ern sector, including Gilgit, Baltistan, Nagir, Hunza, and Yasin, districts in the mountainous regions. Hunza and Baltistan border on China's Sinkiang province.

The war was stalemated at this point. Neither side was able to make progress, and both were glad to let the United Nations effect a ceasefire on January 5, 1949. This left Jammu and Kashmir divided geographically almost in half, although India held the richest and most populous portions.

At this point, the future of Pakistan appeared bleak indeed. Afghanistan was urging the Pathans of the Northwest Frontier province to revolt, and to set up an independent state around the Khyber Pass region. There were rumblings of revolt in Baluchistan. Karachi and the Punjab were jammed with restless refugees. Government politicians were fighting each other for power. And bigoted religious fanatics were stirring up turmoil over the question of how much religious law should be included in their Constitution. The *Jama'at-i-Islami* movement demanded that the Constitution should declare that Pakistan was the agent of God on earth, that religious law would be the supreme law of the land, and that only "true" Moslems could hold public office in the country. Like so many other religions, Islam has a number of sects but the *Jama'at-i-Islami* believed themselves the only true Moslems. Fulfillment of this demand would have made them the only people with a vote in Pakistan.

Other sects, factions, and special-interest groups had their own demands. Together, they kept any Constitution from being written. Liaquat Ali Khan governed under the old British civil law, and he fought hard to bring some discipline into the Moslem League and the country. He was making progress toward that end, when he was assassinated on October 16, 1951, during a speech in Rawalpindi. The killing, although never solved, was attributed to disgruntled political elements in Pakistan.

Nizamuddin, the powerless governor-general, now became prime minister, but he remained powerless. The finance minister, Ghulam Mohammed, assumed the governor-general position and the true power of command. The political situation worsened. Religious riots, disorders over the government's inability to settle the Kashmir problem, and continual substandard living conditions throughout the country, combined to force the resignation of Nizamuddin, and then the removal of Ghulam Mohammed.

Ghulam's downfall came because of East Pakistan. The Bengalis in East Pakistan complained that, although they produced the major per cent of products to earn foreign exchange, most of the money was being spent by the government for the benefit of West Pakistan. Another grievance was that the national capital in West Pakistan was controlled by West Pakistanis. The Bengalis felt they were being treated like a colony, instead of the senior partner with a greater population than West Pakistan. The resentment showed itself when the first Bengali elections were held in March, 1954, and the Moslem League elected only 10 of the 309 East Pakistan assemblymen.

Conditions in both East and West Pakistan became so bad that Ghulam, fearful of being deposed, dissolved the General Assembly and tried to establish himself as a dictator. When he was forced to resign in 1955, he was replaced by "strong man" Iskander Mirza, an army general.

Mirza was an honest man who earnestly tried to bring order out of the growing chaos, but he was also a general who tried to rule as if he were directing an army, instead of a nation of oppressed, starving, and rebellious people. He did succeed in giving Pakistan its first Constitution, and he developed a five-year economic plan to increase industrial activity. He also tried, without any great success, to hold elections under the new system.

Mirza was hampered by different political parties, struggling for power, by food riots in both West and East Pakistan, by dissatisfaction among oppressed farmers, and by the necessity of spending too much of the national budget for defense. This left little money for economic development and welfare. The defense budget was necessary, of course, for India was hungrily waiting, just across the border, to destroy the struggling nation.

The situation was so bad in both West and East Pakistan that General Ayub Khan, commander of the Pakistan army, forced Mirza to suspend the Constitution, dismiss the assembly, disband all political parties, and declare martial law. Ayub Khan was then appointed chief, martial law administrator.

Despite all the censure heaped upon him, in later years, Ayub Khan had been reluctant to seize power in Pakistan. Twice before, he had had the opportunity. In fact, Ghulam Mohammed—seeing his own downfall approaching—had begged Ayub to take over the government before Mirza's rule. Ayub had refused, because his British army training had taught him that soldiers should be aloof from politics. When he finally did accept the post of martial law administrator, and Mirza had been deposed as head of the government, it was because Ayub sincerely believed that the country was in danger of collapse.

Ayub Khan was 51 years old at the time. He was six-feet tall, and looked like a soldier, complete with clipped British moustache. He viewed politics with contempt and was not suited to running a country. He had been born in a village in the Pathan hill country in 1907. He left there to attend the university in Lahore and then obtained an appointment to Great Britain's military academy at Sandhurst. He served with the British Army in Burma and fought the Japanese in World War II. As one of the few top-quality officers, he rose quickly in the Pakistani army after separation and became commander-in-chief.

Ayub began his regime by frankly admitting that his takeover was illegal under the Constitution. "My authority is *force!*" he said. And force he used in a slashing attack on his country's worst problems. He appointed military officers to head most of the major divisions of the government, and he gave them specific orders on what to do. Filth was cleaned out of the major cities. House-by-house searches by military squads uncovered millions of pounds of hoarded rice and grain. One raid discovered two tons of smuggled gold; another resulted in the arrest of two thousand black marketeers.

Price controls went into effect. Thousands of refugees, who had been living as squatters in Karachi since partition, were resettled on land taken from large landowners as part of land reform. He also removed about 1,500 civil service employees whom he considered either corrupt or incompetent.

Ayub Khan, while bringing badly needed order to Pakistan, was a dictator in every sense of the word. He kept the ban on political parties and ruthlessly suppressed all opposition to his regime. He appointed a commission to draft a new Constitution for the country, but he rejected the commission's suggestions and ended up in writing the new Constitution himself with the aid of two friends. The National Assembly was limited to a single house, but provided for two provincial assemblies for local government of West and East Pakistan. The president was given extraordinary powers. He could issue laws in his own name, good for six months, if the National Assembly did not happen to be in session. But if he decided there was a national emergency, he could personally issue laws that would stay in force indefinitely.

It appeared at this point that Ayub Khan, despite the political repression, was just the man Pakistan had needed since the death of Quaid-i-Azam Ali Jinnah. Unfortunately, the Pakistan situation was beyond the ability of any man to solve.

CHAPTER 11

Pakistan and the World

In contrast to India, Pakistan, did not enlist much world sympathy, during its first troublesome decade of life. India was a word and country the world knew. Pakistan was unfamiliar and seemingly of little interest to countries like the United States who virtually ignored Pakistan, while concentrating on trying to win India's friendship.

This changed suddenly in 1954 when the cold war between the United States and Russia reached the point where the United States decided that, unless she insured the alignment of Pakistan with the West, the country would move into the Russian orbit. Indeed, Russia was already making overtures to the Pakistani government. Iskander Mirza, who was still president, wanted powerful foreign allies as protection from possible Indian aggression. He discussed the matter with Ayub Khan, who was then commander-in-chief of the army. They both feared Russian influence in their country and, considering the lavishness with which the United States was then handing out military aid to its friends, they decided that Pakistan's best interest lay with the West.

Mirza had Pakistan join SEATO—the Southeast Asia Treaty Organization—which the United States had sponsored as a protective buffer against Russian expansion in Southeast Asia. Free U.S. military equipment immediately began to pour into Pakistan. By 1968 this had amounted to more than two-and-a-half billion dollars, according to the *Pakistan Economic Survey*, published by Pakistan's Ministry of Finance. This accounted for just about half of the entire foreign aid that the country had received during those years. After 1955, an enormous amount of help had poured into the country, much of it grant aid which it was not necessary to repay. Foreign loans finally reached a total of more than a billion U.S. dollars. Many other countries that extended aid did so in the form of supplies. Project aid accounted for a large amount of foreign assistance to Pakistan. This was made available mainly in the form of capital goods and technical services. The aid was given in order to expand efficiency and output in agriculture, transportation, irrigation, power, and industry.

American military aid to Pakistan infuriated Nehru. In a speech in Delhi, the Indian prime minister accused Pakistan of importing the East-West cold war into the Indian subcontinent. He tried to get other Southeast Asian nations to break relations with Pakistan because of its military pact with the United States. Pakistan retorted that Nehru's desire was for a weak neighbor that he could eventually reabsorb by aggression, similar to the seizure of so much of Kashmir and Jammu.

One of the results of American aid to Pakistan was the development of a supersecret airport at Peshawar. It was to be used by the U.S. spy plane, the U-2, for reconnaissance flights over Russia. These lightweight, extremely long-winged planes could achieve remarkably high altitudes. It was thought, at the time, that they were able to fly above any possible Russian missile. In 1960, the world was electrified by evidence that Russian heat-seeking missiles had knocked down an American U-2, during a spy flight over Russia. The pilot, Gary Francis Powers, a civilian, was placed on trial in Moscow to the accompaniment of a barrage of anti-American propaganda. In the course of the trial, it was revealed that the planes were using bases in Turkey and Pakistan to shuttle across Russia. This brought a Russian threat to bomb American bases in Pakistan.

American foreign policy has an unfortunate tendency to shift radically with changes in administration. Friendship with the United States often is merely friendship with a particular president and his advisers. His successor may or may not follow the same policies. The initial U.S. rapport and military treaties with Pakistan were negotiated by the Eisenhower administration, during a period of intense fear of Russia. The U.S. policy then was to build a ring of military bases around Russia. This ring would include the five NATO nations, plus Turkey, Japan, Thailand, Pakistan, and others.

This policy was continued by the Kennedy Administration that followed Eisenhower, but with decreasing emphasis. The big publicity event in those years was the visit of Vice President Lyndon B. Johnson to Pakistan. In the course of his visit, Johnson stopped to talk to a Pakistani camel driver, Bashir Ahmed. In his typical Texas manner, the vice president told Bashir to drop in and see him at the LBJ ranch in Texas. Bashir looked upon this as an invitation, and eventually a private group financed a trip to the United States for the camel driver. He was also presented with a pickup truck to replace his camel cart.

Then, in 1961, Pakistani President Ayub Khan made a goodwill trip to Washington and Mrs. John F. Kennedy made a trip to Pakistan the following year. But United States-Pakistan relations suffered a setback, later in 1962, as a direct result of trouble between China and India over a disputed border. Communist Chinese troops occupied the disputed territory. India considered

Pakistan to be the greater threat, and therefore would not remove troops on duty at the Pakistan-India border to bolster her forces facing the Chinese.

India's fear was that military involvement with the Chinese would give Pakistan an opportunity to drive India out of Kashmir. Zulfikar Ali Bhutto, a dynamic young lawyer who had been appointed foreign minister, was as much alarmed by British and U.S. military aid to India at this time as Nehru had been to the original Pakistan-U.S. military pact. Pakistan, while still receiving U.S. aid although in decreasing quantities, began to look for other foreign friends. Russia was out of the question, because of Pakistan's earlier decision to side with the United States in the cold war. Bhutto and Ayub took the position that any enemy of India was a potential friend of Pakistan. Consequently, Bhutto made overtures to China.

American government officials, realizing their mistake, tried to reassure Pakistan, but it was too late to stop Pakistan's move toward some kind of rapport with China. Earlier, Pakistan had joined SEATO—the Southeast Asia Treaty Organization—which the United States had sponsored to contain China's expansion in Asia. But Pakistan had done this to gain American support, and not because she feared Chinese aggression. In seeking China's friendship now, Bhutto could point out that Pakistan had been among the first nations to recognize the Communist government, when it took control of China in 1949. Later, Pakistan had supported China's claim to the seat in the United Nations held by Chiang Kai-shek's Nationalist Chinese Government in Taiwan. This resulted in a definite improvement in Chinese-Pakistan relations. The two nations, sharing a common border in the Hunza and Balistan states in the Himalayas, amicably settled their own border dispute. India, on the other hand, absolutely refused to compromise, thus moving to the brink of war.

The tensions eased temporarily, but exploded in war in September, 1965. Several events of alarming portent preceded the actual outbreak of war. In December, 1963 a human hair, claimed to be from the head of the Prophet Mohammed, was stolen from a Moslem temple in Kashmir. The theft was blamed on the Hindus and riots ensued. This turn of events greatly alarmed the Indian government, and matters worsened in January, 1964, when retaliatory anti-Moslem riots flared up in Calcutta. They were almost as bad as those that shook the city, during the fateful days of the partition.

When Kashmir first fell to India, immediately after Partition, Sheikh Abdullah, because of his hatred of Ali Jinnah, had chosen to cooperate with the Indians. Abdullah, a Moslem, was the only political leader with sufficient charisma to guide the confused Kashmiri. Later, when Abdullah had not proved as amenable as Nehru desired, he was jailed. Now the Indians rushed to free Abdullah from confinement, for they knew he was the only person who could prevent further bloodshed in Kashmir. The "hair of the prophet" was returned, and conditions settled into an uneasy peace.

Nehru was badly shaken. The Indian prime minister, himself a native of Kashmir, had hoped to convince the Kashmiris that religion made no difference in the new India. The latest riots, however, clearly showed that the old animosity was as strong as ever. In addition, the military confrontation with China the previous year had proved that his policy of nonalignment was not working. Accordingly, Nehru had been forced to accept heavy military aid from both the United States and Great Britain. He now hinted that India might soften her demands on Kashmir. But before anything concrete could be put into motion, Nehru died on May 27, 1964.

Lal Bahadur Shastri became the new prime minister. It was Shastri's avowed intention to continue Nehru's new policy of trying to find some way to ease the tension between India and Pakistan. But swiftly moving events were beyond his control. Immediately, India and Pakistan troops were shooting at each other in the Rann of Kutch area. This section on the edge of the Thar Desert, between Indian and Pakastani land on the Arabian Sea, is a desolate, unlivable region of scorching stretches of land in summer and salt marshes in winter. India claimed that Pakistan was trying to fortify the area. Pakistan insisted that India wanted the region as a launching base for a direct attack on Karachi.

The matter was settled after a few shots were fired, but trouble of far greater magnitude exploded in Kashmir later in the year. Sheikh Abdullah, after being released from prison in Kashmir, had been given an Indian passport to permit him to make a *haj* (pilgrimage) to Mecca, the holy Moslem city in Arabia. Going beyond Mecca, Abdullah visited Algiers in order to see Chou En-lai, the Chinese premier, who was visiting North Africa. In view of Pakistan's new rapport with China, India regarded this meeting as something sinister. Abdullah's Indian passport was promptly withdrawn, and he was ordered to return to Kashmir. Pakistan immediately offered the Kashmiri leader a Pakistan passport, but Abdullah refused. Instead, he returned to India where he was arrested and imprisoned in the south of the country. It had been a calculated risk on his part, for he felt he would draw more support from his Kashmiri people as an Indian prisoner than as an exiled fugitive.

The Kashmiri Moslems then began to form guerrilla bands to harrass the Indians. Riots tore Srinagar, the Kashmiri capital, and quickly spread to other Indian-held cities. Major fighting broke out on the cease-fire line, between Pakistan and Indian-held Kashmir. Pakistan volunteers, following the policy during the fighting in 1947, began to infilter from Pakistan into Kashmir in order to join in the struggle.

Suddenly, without prior notice or declaration of war, the Indian army rolled across the cease-fire line into Pakistan territory on August 15th. This could have been interpreted simply as a military action to protect Indian positions from guerrilla attacks. But, on September 6, 1965, two Indian armored columns crossed the Pakistan border on a direct thrust toward Lahore, the ancient cultural city of Pakistan. A third column then crossed the border for an attack on Sialkot in Pakistan. Air attacks were simultaneously launched on Pakistani air fields.

The fighting quickly developed into a stalemate when neither side was able to advance. The United States—hitherto a principal supplier of arms to both India and Pakistan—cut off all further shipments of munitions. Great Britain, who had supplied the bulk of India's aircraft and tanks, also threatened to stop shipments. Neither Russia nor China wanted war on the Indian subcontinent. The major countries then turned to the United Nations to end the war. U Thant, the Burmese diplomat then serving as secretary-general of the UN, went to Delhi and Rawalpindi (the temporary Pakistani capital), after the UN Security Council voted for an immediate cease-fire.

Lal Bahadur Shastri replied that India would welcome a ceasefire, but only if Pakistan withdrew from Kashmir. Ayub Khan, in turn, demanded that all Indian and Pakistani troops be withdrawn from Kashmir and replaced by UN troops, who would oversee a free election within three months. Originally, Pakistan had been against a free election to decide Kashmir's future because of the coolness that existed between Sheikh Abdullah and Ali Jinnah. Now, however, they felt that Abdullah would favor union with Pakistan.

Neither Pakistan nor India would agree to the other's conditions, and U Thant reported his failure to the Security Council. A new resolution, supported by the United States, Russia, France, England, and Nationalist China (the then five permanent members of the Security Council), demanded a cease-fire by September 22, 1965 and a return to the cease-fire line, established in 1949. Both Pakistan and India gave in, and the cease-fire went into effect on September 23rd.

Communist China had been the only country that gave direct aid to Pakistan during this crisis. This had come in the form of a renewal of the China-India border dispute which put pressure on India, during the delicate negotiation period. Pakistan felt that she had been badly let down by her international friends in this time of extreme crisis. And so Ayub Khan was receptive when Russia, after years of favoring India, suddenly made friendly overtures to Pakistan. Russian Prime Minister Kosygin arranged for Pakistan and India to meet at Tashkent, Russia, for a conference chaired by Kosygin himself. The objective was to try and settle Pakistan-India problems.

After several failures, Pakistani Foreign Minister Bhutto and Indian Prime Minister Lal Bahadur Shastri worked out a basic agreement. It carefully ignored the future of Kashmir, required both sides to withdraw to the former cease-fire line and to repatriate prisoners of war; also to resume full diplomatic relations and to continue discussions aimed at settling long-standing subjects of hostility. Shastri died of a heart attack on January 10, 1966, the day following the signing of this agreement. Since that time, the Kashmir question has remained dormant, although Z.A. Bhutto (now president of Pakistan), in his recent speeches, has shown signs of stirring it up again.

While diplomatically desirable for both India and Pakistan, since they were at a military stalemate, the Tashkent agreement was not popular with warring factions in either India or Pakistan. Like so many settlements that do not erase basic causes of the problem, this situation was an invitation to later complications. When trouble finally came in 1971, the tragedy matched the terror and bloodshed of partition in 1947.

The decision to stop fighting in 1966 was unpopular and worked against the regime of President Ayub Khan. Ayub began his dictatorship with a zeal to clean up corruption and put the government on a sound footing. However, as time passed, cracks began to appear in the shining armor of the reform government. Incompetent and corrupt civil service employees, dismissed by Ayub, were replaced by his supporters who proved no better than those that had been ousted. The much hailed land reform proved to be only a myth. The huge landowners only lost a small part of their property; graft and corruption, after an initial lessening, returned in full force. Ayub, like all reform leaders, found that it was possible to clean out corruption of opponents, but impossible to stop similar activities of his supporters. One must have supporters in order to stay in power, but, unfortunately, they invariably demand their pound of public flesh to make it worth their while. Apparently, true patriotism and regard for the general welfare is extremely rare.

Opposition to Ayub's worsening regime increased after the Indo-Pakistan War of 1965. Hundreds of political opponents were jailed, including the dynamic Z.A. Bhutto who had been Ayub's foreign minister. In East Pakistan, the popular leader, Sheikh Mujibur Rahman, was also jailed for inciting opposition to Ayub. Conditions were approaching chaos in East Pakistan which was ruled by Ayub as if it were merely a province, rather than the most populated portion of Pakistan. The Bengalis of East Pakistan were being bled economically by the diversion of their foreign exchange to build up West Pakistan, instead of their own section—a cause of great discontent.

One of the drains on foreign exchange was Ayub's insistence on building a new capital at Islamabad, 10 miles from Rawalpindi in the Punjab. A beautiful city was planned, but critics protested that government favorites in industry and in the army were making fortunes in land speculation and buildings in the new city. Moreover, twenty-two family groups were accused of holding a major percentage of the country's industry. It was claimed that government-built industries—many constructed with aid funds—were sold to one or the other of these families at prices worth only a third of their true value.

Student riots, strikes in major industries, and general unrest, shook both East and West Pakistan. Bhutto, correctly judging the temper of the people, moved toward the left and declared for "Islamic Socialism." Desperately seeking to hold his crumbling regime together, Ayub ordered martial law. But, unfortunately, although he had been commander-in-chief of the army, his ten years as dictator had permitted new commanders with their own supporters to rise up in the army. The present commander-in-chief, Yahya Khan, did not believe that bolstering his one-time friend, Ayub, would help at all. In fact, Yahya was sure it would

The General Assembly Hall

plunge the country into full civil war. Although Bhutto's Pakistan People's Party in the West and Mujibur Rahman's Awami League in the East were strongly against Ayub, the real opposition was not centered in any political party. Rather, it sprang from the total masses of people in both sectors of Pakistan.

As 1968 drew to a close, the country was paralyzed by industrial strikes and a student strike and riot in Dacca, East Pakistan's capital. Earlier in the year, a student in Peshawar had tried to assassinate Ayub, while the prime minister was delivering a speech in the famous Khyber Pass area of the city.

In February, 1969, in an attempt to lessen disorders in Dacca, Ayub released Mujibur Rahman from jail. The East Pakistan leader immediately challenged the national government with his famous "Six Points." The basic complaint of East Pakistan was that it was not an equal partner in the government and did not have full control of its own province. The Six Points, summarized below, attempted to correct the imbalances:

1. A Federal parliament, which would be elected by universal adult vote, and would be the supreme power of the nation.
2. West and East Pakistan would be equal, federated states with total power to conduct their own affairs, except for defense and foreign policy.
3. Separate fiscal policies—even separate currencies, if necessary—to prevent withdrawal of capital from East Pakistan to West Pakistan.
4. All taxes would be raised by the two states. These states would give the federal government such funds as were necessary for defense and general expenses.
5. Each of the two states would have authority to make separate trade agreements with foreign nations.
6. The states would have authority to raise their own militia.

In effect, Mujibur's Six Points would create two individual nations, held together only by their common religion and defense, and by a shared foreign policy. A similar plan had been suggested and defeated in the United States, when it was struggling to form a strong government after the Revolutionary War. However, the theory of "states' rights" was not settled until the American Civil War, many years later.

The situation was rapidly degenerating into total anarchy. Yahya Khan finally took action on March 25, 1969. Like Ayub, Yahya was a professional soldier who had served with distinction with the British Indian Army in World War II. He had been trained in the tradition that soldiers held themselves aloof from politics. But now he felt that he had no choice, for martial law was the only recourse that could prevent anarchy.

Yahya Khan began—like Ayub before him—as martial law administrator, but shortly after proclaimed himself president. In a speech to the nation, he forcefully told his people that he was acting to save the country from utter destruction. He then laid down some harsh rules to restore order. Yahya declared that he would not tolerate strikes or rioting and would prescribe strong punishment for violators. He said that creating disorder, undermining government authority, and blackmarketing, were crimes against all the people.

"My sole aim" he stated, "is to protect the lives, liberty and property of the people, and to put the administration of government back on the rails. I have no ambition other than this."

Order was restored almost magically. Yahya Khan inspired respect in the people, for the opposition parties realized the danger the country faced. India was sitting on the frontier, hungrily awaiting an excuse to reabsorb Pakistan.

Moving against corruption Yahya scheduled the country's first free election. But, at the same time, there were rumblings under the surface that indicated that those who supported Yahya were not as patriotically minded as he presumed. These rumblings of discontent would soon erupt into the gravest crisis in Pakistan's history.

East Against West

Yahya Khan sincerely believed that he could solve Pakistan's problems, but his hopes were destroyed by three factors. One was the greed of the group upon whom he had to depend for the political and military power he needed to stay in office. The second factor was the violent hatred of East Pakistan for West Pakistan. Religion was the sole tie between the two Pakistans, and it was insufficient to make up for the years of political and economic neglect of East Pakistan's drastic problems. The third factor in Yahya Khan's failure was his own unshakable belief that force was the basic solution to Pakistan's rumbling political situation.

East Pakistan rallied behind the leadership of Mujibur Rahman. Mindful that East Pakistan's population exceeded that of West Pakistan, Mujibur pushed hard for free elections—"one man, one vote." He was well aware that this would place the government of Pakistan in the hands of his Awami League Party. The seat of power, and possibly the government itself, would then shift from West Pakistan to East Pakistan. Because East Pakistan had been exploited for the benefit of West Pakistan, ever since the union had been formed, this would be economically disasterous for West Pakistan.

Yahya Khan was committed to a free election, but at the same time he had to find some means of preventing the 55 per cent majority in East Pakistan from overthrowing his own government in a free election. Yahya's course of action was to make promises and then procrastinate. He agreed that East and West Pakistan should be on an equal status with maximum autonomy in the conduct of their internal affairs. But he insisted that none of this should be permitted to break down the solidity of the nation. The two Pakistans had to remain strongly tied together; as divided entities, they would be at the mercy of a vengeful India.

The new dictator moved swiftly to show his sincerity. Over 300 corrupt army officers and more than 1,000 civil service people were removed. He increased minimum wages for factory workers and the right to strike was restored. Government restrictions on colleges were removed; then, to show his good faith, Yahya pardoned students who had been jailed in East Pakistan for political demonstrations in violation of Yahya Khan's initial martial law regulations.

Despite opposition from the twenty-two influential families (the reputed controllers of Pakistan's economy), Yahya Khan announced in August, 1969, that voter lists would be prepared, and the country's first fully free election would be held in October, 1970. Yahya stipulated that the voters would also select a committee to frame a new Constitution which the Constitutional Committee would have 120 days to produce. If it failed, the committee would be dissolved, and there would be new elections. All this was cause for apprehension in West Pakistan and jubilation in East Pakistan.

In March, 1970, on the anniversary of his assumption of power, Yahya presented details of his plan to return the government to civilian control. The National Assembly would have 300 elected seats. East Pakistan would have 162, and West Pakistan would have 138—the division being made on the basis of their respective populations. Additional autonomy would be given to the provinces, but a strong central government would be retained. The Constitution would be Islamic, establishing Islam as the national religion. At the same time, Yahya repeated what he had said when he assumed power the previous year. He did not wish to lead the country any longer than necessary. He was a soldier and wanted to return to the army.

The announcement of the coming elections set off a frenzy of political maneuvering. Speculation centered on Zulfikar Ali Bhutto in the West and Mujibur Rahman in the East. Bhutto had been a minister in Ayub Khan's government until he broke away to form his own People's Party in 1967. Bhutto was then a young lawyer, extremely dynamic and extroverted. He had broken with Ayub Khan over the Tashkent Treaty which Bhutto felt gave India too much. In 1966, he had visited Dacca in East Pakistan, and later called this region "the most important part of Pakistan." Still later, after he formed his socialistic People's Party, Bhutto said that he supported East Pakistan's demand for self-government. He was enormously popular in West Pakistan, and it was thought that this attitude might win Bhutto's People's Party enough votes in East Pakistan for him to carry the election. However, Bhutto was hurt by his inability to come to any kind of an agreement with Mujibur Rahman who was popularly called "Sheikh Mujib," although he had never been a chief.

Rahman was born in a small village in 1919 of a family with sufficient means to send him to Calcutta's Islamia College. He was a poor student, but showed early signs of being a brilliant organizer. He was a student in Dacca's University Law School when Pakistan was formed. Immediately, he jumped into the political fight and was expelled for his "radical" activity. In 1949,

In times of floods, which come regularly every year, the fortunate are those who make their homes on boats.

he helped to reform the Awami League which was then Communist-dominated, more Maoist in nature than Russian. During the next few years, Mujibur Rahman was continually jailed for subversion. At the same time, his popularity and influence increased in East Pakistan. His rising power in East Pakistan politics climaxed in his famous "Six Points" demand on the Ayub government. When Yahya Khan had taken over, East Pakistan was in a state of complete anarchy, and it was entirely due to Mujibur Rahman that order was restored. Now the East Pakistanis eagerly awaited the election that would at last, they felt, give them control of the country.

In West Pakistan, there was frantic maneuvering to find a way to stall the elections. Yahya Khan had been forced to agree to hold them, so as to restore order in East Pakistan. Then Nature provided him with the excuse for postponement that West Pakistan sought.

Bengal, the Indian province from which East Pakistan was carved, is a low alluvial plain formed by silt from the mighty Brahmaputra River and Ganges River systems. The land itself is split by literally thousands of streams feeding into these two great rivers. During the monsoon season, East Pakistan suffered from tremendous floods when the streams failed to carry away the torrents of rain. Floods came regularly each year, but the monsoon of August, 1970, was the worst in fifty years. The torrential rains flooded an area of 15,000 square miles, sweeping away a quarter-million homes and destroying $200 million in crops. The entire region was turned into one gigantic swamp.

Yahya Khan flew to Dacca, capital of East Pakistan, to personally assess the damage which engulfed one half of the province. It was obviously impossible to hold an election under these frightful circumstances. Accordingly, Yahya announced that the elections would be postponed until December. Some of the government's critics denounced the delay, but the majority realized that, if half of the Bengali Pakistanis were physically unable to vote, it would not be representative election.

As the sodden Bengalis dug themselves out of the mud, the various political parties redoubled their campaign efforts for the crucial December elections. Engrossed as they were in both campaigning and relief work, the Bengalis took little interest in an announcement that an American weather satellite had spotted a storm moving up the Bay of Bengal. The storm, with head winds of 100 miles an hour, was expected to hit the Indian coast, but on November 10th, it changed direction and pointed directly toward the Ganges delta region of East Pakistan. It increased in fury, the winds now reaching 150 miles per hour.

Storm warnings were issued, but there had been similar warnings a few weeks previously that had not proven necessary. Therefore, no one paid much attention this time. In fact, there was little they could have done, even if the warning had been carried into the backwaters. The mouths of the Ganges River had created more than 200 little islands in the delta, where the river empties into the Bay of Bengal. Most of these were small, low-lying, and little more than overgrown sand bars. They were dangerous places to make homes, for every storm inundated them. However, India and East Pakistan are so crowded that hungry people seek any sort of ground where they can grow a bit of food to keep their families from starving.

The cyclonic storm struck the unsuspecting islanders with colossal fury, sweeping away the shacks, uprooting trees, and drowning thousands. The resulting tidal wave reached 25 feet in height, as it smashed across the delta region and inundated the coasts on both the east and west shores of the narrow upper reaches of the Bay of Bengal. The storm moved inland, gradually losing force, but leaving behind catastrophic destruction.

The delta islands were struck at midnight on a Thursday. It was Sunday before the full extent of the damage filtered into the East Pakistan Government in Dacca. The government was totally unable to cope with a catastrophe of such enormous proportions. Yahya Khan had been in Peking on a state visit when the disaster struck. He diverted his return to visit East Pakistan, flying over the stricken area. The president took a fatalistic view, proclaiming, "It is the will of Allah." His enemies immediately accused him of a callous attitude and criminal neglect to act during East Pakistan's gravest crisis.

In the meantime, death reports reached enormous figures. One report claimed that 190,000 had been drowned in a single area. People and animals lay rotting along the water-logged shores, threatening to add pestilence and plague to the overwhelming burden of the miserable survivors.

The British Government moved first and was most effective in rushing in aid. A task force was flown up from Singapore. British Marines began to bury the Moslem dead and to cremate the Hindu victims. Other foreign countries—India, the United States, the International Red Cross, and some United Nations agencies, also gave aid in varying amounts. The Pakistani Air Force refused to permit Indian Air Force helicopters to join the rescue work on grounds that they were "spies."

No one ever knew how many people were actually killed because most of the corpses were quickly rolled into nameless graves to avoid epidemics. Estimates have run as high as a million, but informed sources put the figure at about half a million. Several reporters called it "one of the greatest natural disasters of modern times."

At first, Mujibur Rahman refused to make any comment, but later he lashed out at the Pakistan Government for what he called criminal neglect. "Our rulers have been tardy and callous," he charged. "The textile millionaires have not given a yard of cloth for our shrouds. The government has a huge army, but left the British Marines the job of burying our dead."

Yahya struck back by claiming that he had done his "damndest," adding, "we did the best that could be done." He accused Bengali politicians of spreading false tales to arouse hatred of West Pakistan. Others truthfully pointed out that relief food was turned into a political weapon, and Awami supporters were getting preference. Local officials demanded bribes before they would distribute relief supplies, and much of the medical deliveries were diverted into the black market.

At the same time, left-wing critics assailed those who offered the most help. Great Britain's direct contributions and splendid job of relief left critics of the West with nothing to complain about, so they attacked the British on other grounds. British aid, they said, had just been a publicity stunt to prove that their help was still needed in the land they once governed.

Strangely, the criticism even hit Pope Paul who had stopped in Dacca en route to the Philippines to give President Yahya a check for $10,000 to help relief efforts. One writer suggested this was nothing but a publicity stunt for the Catholic Church. Criticism of the government reached such proportions that Yahya Khan did not think it expedient to again postpone the elections. He announced that they would be held in December, except in the nine East Pakistan provinces where rehabilitation was still going on. However, he promised elections would be held in these areas later.

The elections went off as scheduled, and despite the criticism of the opposition, they were fairly conducted. Both sides admitted as much, but few gave credit to Yahya. There were 56 million registered voters, and 40 million turned out at the polls; 153 seats were allotted to East Pakistan, and Mujibur Rahman's Awami Party took 151 of them. The West Pakistan allotment was 138 seats and Bhutto's People Party took 81. Yahya made a public statement in which he called Mujibur the "next prime minister of Pakistan."

In retrospect, Yahya Khan had acted up to this point in what seemed the very best interests of Pakistan. He had saved the country from anarchy, had uprooted some of the corruption, and had given the Pakistanis their first truly free election. Now he tried to carry out the rest of his promise to the people. He called Bhutto and Mujibur together to try and get them to work out some kind of agreement on the proposed Constitution. Mujibur flatly refused to compromise in any way whatsoever. He insisted that the Constitution must be based upon his "Six Points." This would primarily mean complete autonomy for East Pakistan with the right to self-government, coinage of its own money, handling its own foreign affairs, and raising its own militia, among other demands.

Yahya and Bhutto protested that this would create an independent nation of East Pakistan, and thus would destroy the union. Both weakened countries would then be at the mercy of India. Mujibur retorted that instead of weakening Pakistan this would strengthen the nation, but he failed to explain how this would happen. Mujibur wanted a loose federation something like the American Colonies had, before the adoption of the U.S. Constitution; that is, a loose federation of independent states with a weak federal government.

Yahya Khan was somewhat in the same position as that of Abraham Lincoln, just before the outbreak of the American Civil War. He had the difficult job of trying to prevent the breakup of the Pakistan union. His determination was fully supported by Bhutto and the Pakistani army generals. When Mujibur Rahman and his supporters were equally determined not to give in, the stalemate moved swiftly toward its tragic climax.

At this point, Tajuddin Ahmed, Mujibur Rahman's associate, announced that the Awami Party did not need the cooperation of Bhutto's People's Party or the participation of President Yahya Khan. "We won the election," he asserted. "We have a clear mandate from the people. We will frame our own Constitution and form our own central government."

Bhutto replied that no one party would be permitted to force upon the entire nation its own Constitution, and that if the Awami Party tried to do so, "the People's Party will not be responsible for what happens next."

Yahya Khan realized that his promise of turning over the military government to civilian control was now impossible. The East Pakistanis were determined to split the union, and he was equally determined to maintain it. However, he kept working hard to bring together Bhutto in the West and Mujibur Rahman in the East. Agitation was becoming more open in Dacca for an independent East Pakistan, under the name of Bangladesh (Land of the Bengalis), so he prudently began to reinforce the Pakistani army in East Pakistan.

Despite the censure that engulfed him later, Yahya Khan, earnestly worked to divert the coming explosion. He went to Dacca to talk to Mujibur Rahman, when the Sheikh refused to come to West Pakistan, and then persuaded Z.A. Bhutto to go to East Pakistan for a conference. Bhutto had to be protected by armed guards to keep him from being mobbed by the aroused Bengalis.

At this point, Yahya realized that the East Pakistanis were determined to break free of the Pakistan union. Nothing but force could prevent dissolution of the nation. He replaced pro-Bengali Vice Admiral Ahsan, governor of East Pakistan, with tough, Bengali-hating General Tikka Khan and announced that the constitutional assembly had been postponed indefinitely. At the same time, he dismissed his ten-member civilian cabinet (of whom five were Bengalis) and established martial law.

On March 1, 1971, Yahya Khan went on the radio to explain his actions to the nation and to ask for support. He blamed the delay in opening the National Assembly on the political parties. Once again, he insisted that he could not turn over the government to one party and allow it to dictate terms of a Constitution for the entire nation. Yahya acknowledged that the delay put the country in the gravest crisis, but he hoped that it would give the stubborn politicians time to work out the deadlock. Again he promised that he would end martial law and turn over power to duly elected officials, just as soon as conditions warranted.

East Pakistan exploded with violence. It began with a five-day strike that brought all business to a standstill. Mobs of demonstrators jammed the streets of Dacca, shouting, "Joi Bangla!" ("Victory to Bengal!"). Mobs attacked and looted all non-Bengali stores. English language signs were torn down. Hindus and West

Pakistanis in East Pakistan were attacked. Dacca was under mob rule for a week, and by March 6th more than 3,000 people had been slaughtered by the vengeful mobs. Dacca International Airport was jammed with terror-stricken West Pakistanis trying to get out of the city. Foreign governments flew in their own aircraft to rescue their embassy personnel.

Strangely, the Pakistani Army, under the control of Yahya Khan, did not try to control the mobs. Yahya's supporters claimed that this was proof of the president's sincerity in trying to work out a peaceful settlement of the crisis. Yahya's enemies later charged that he had permitted the mob to commit excesses in order to excuse the army's excesses later on.

Mujibur Rahman now moved toward partial control of the mobs, and ordered shops to open and sell food. At the same time, he flatly rejected an invitation to meet with Bhutto and Yahya Khan. The president made still another attempt to hold the nation together, when he agreed to let the elected assembly meet on March 25th. In a speech to the nation, he declared again that he would not be instrumental in a partition of Pakistan. "Let there be no doubt on this," he said. "I have a duty to both the people of East and West Pakistan to preserve this country. I will not let a handful of people destroy our homeland."

In East Pakistan, the people had gone too far to draw back. They were demanding independence now. Mujibur Rahman scheduled a talk the day following President Yahya Khan's last declaration. The preceding night, demonstrators had filled the streets, shouting, "Joi Bangla!" They were certain that on the morrow Mujibur would announce East Pakistan's withdrawal from the Pakistan union and the formation of the nation of Bangladesh.

Mujibur had warned his supporters that an attempt to declare East Pakistan independence would cost a million lives. But now no one seemed to care. All they could think of was "Joi Bangla!" —"Victory to Bengal!"

CHAPTER 13

Blood and Terror

The mobs of Dacca were still shouting, "Joi Bangla," as they jammed the city to hear Sheikh Mujibur Rahman reply to President Yahya Khan. They—and Yahya, too—expected the East Pakistan leader to declare his sector's independence and the creation of the nation of Bangladesh.

But the Sheikh stopped short of independence. Instead, he renewed his demands that the army—predominantly made up of West Pakistanis—be withdrawn and that East Pakistan's autonomy be recognized. He promised a massive campaign of civil disobedience, if these demands were not met.

Factories immediately closed and prices soared. The government was paralyzed by Awami League boycotts, and justice stagnated as judges went out on strike with the rest of East Pakistan's civil service. Foreigners began to evacuate the country. United Nations relief work in the cyclone-stricken areas stopped when Secretary General U Thant ordered his personnel to leave, because the government could no longer guarantee their safety. This action affected three million refugees in need of aid.

Yahya Khan made one last effort to come to terms with Mujibur. He and Bhutto went to Dacca where Bhutto was almost mobbed. Pakistan "Republic Day" (Independence Day) came on March 23rd while Bhutto, Yahya, and Mujibur were trying to reach a compromise. The Awami League renamed it "Resistance Day." A Bangladesh flag was raised over Mujibur's home. He made no protest when students gathered there to burn a Pakistani flag and a picture of Ali Jinnah, the Father of Pakistan.

Bhutto and Yahya spent the next day in Dacca, although they realized that it was now impossible to come to terms with Mujibur. On the twenty-fifth of March, without attempting to see the East Pakistani leader again, they quietly left for West Pakistan. Word was then dispatched to the Pakistani army commanders in Dacca to move against the "rebels." The tragedy of Pakistan had come to its climax.

The union of East and West Pakistan had been a mistake from the beginning. The new nation had been torn out of India solely for religious reasons. It did remove the minority Moslem Indians from the domination of the Hindu Indians whom they hated, but at the same time it brought together two groups of Moslems who were actually strangers. In culture, history, and outlook, they were foreigners in each other's eyes. All they had in common was the Islamic religion, and that had failed to weld together such dissimilar peoples.

Dom Moraes, the Indian-born journalist, commented:

> Those who still feel that a religion can unite a country would do well to consider the case of Pakistan. Its founders thought that a poor and backward people would rally to the call of religion more quickly than to the call of nationalism. . . . No-

where can the concept of Islamic brotherhood have been disproved so completely as in Pakistan.

Except for minor clashes, the army had remained passive while the East Pakistani mobs roamed the streets and attacked West Pakistanis, foreigners, and the hated Hindus. But now Yahya Khan freed the soldiers of their restraints. Tanks began to roll through the streets of Dacca around midnight of March 25th. A few hours before, military police had quietly rounded up all foreign newspapermen in Dacca and had taken them to the international airport, where they were deported to Karachi the next morning. This move was a tip-off that drastic military action was being contemplated, and that the government wanted no foreign correspondents to witness what was about to occur. Then all that would be known about the operation would be what the official government communiqués released. However, two reporters managed to elude the military police, and their subsequent stories tell what happened. When the foreign correspondents were removed, all members of the Awami League, except Mujibur Rahman, fled from Dacca.

The army, under orders to stamp out the rebellion in East Pakitan, struck first against students at Dacca University. Machine guns and tank cannon ripped into Iqbal Hall (named for Mohammed Iqbal, one of the founding fathers of Pakistan). Simon Dring of the London *Daily Telegraph* reported:

> Caught completely by surprise, some two hundred students were killed in Iqbal Hall, headquarters of the antigovernment students' union, as shells slammed into the building. . . . Two days later, bodies were still smoldering in their burning rooms, others were scattered outside and more floated in a nearby lake.

After this initial attack, armored companies and infantry fanned out through the city. Awami League newspapers and political headquarters were burned. Hundreds were dragged out and shot. Fires raged throughout the city. While the "rebels" (those members of Mujibur Rahman's Awami League) were the avowed target of the army, within an hour of the attack on Iqbal Hall, the soldiers' fury had turned on the hated Hindus.

The Hindus in Dacca were concentrated in the sector known as "the Old City." This is the area along the Burhiganga River where Dacca was first settled. It is a slum with dilapidated buildings, narrow, winding streets, and frightful overcrowding. The Pakistani Army stormed into the Old City with vengeful fury.

In all fairness to the Pakistani troops, it must be pointed out that they were repeating what had been done to their own people, during the bloody atrocities that followed Partition in 1947. A large number of the soldiers were from Moslem Punjab. They remembered only too well the terror which they and their families had gone through, when the Punjab was split into Pakistani

The "Old City" of Dacca where the Pakistani Army slaughtered so many Hindus in March, 1971, as a prelude to the civil war that came in December of that year. The result was the formation of the new nation of Bangladesh.

and Indian sectors. They remembered the sickening tales told by refugees who streamed out of India and recalled the thousands of Moslems who were slaughtered in Hindu rioting in Calcutta and Bombay. Nothing that happened in Bangladesh was any worse than some of the frightful examples told by Sir Francis Tuker in his account of the Partition atrocities.

Of course, beastiality is no excuse for retaliation in kind. But still, one must consider that these horrors were deeply etched in the minds of the soldiers as they shot, slashed, and burned their way through the terrorized city. While it is true that in 1947 the Pakistanis tried to strike back with terror of their own it is also true that the Pakistanis suffered more than they gave during the frightful period that followed Partition. Apart from their memories of Sikh and Hindu atrocities, the Pakistani soldiers were inflamed by propaganda—a standard technique in any army to give the soldier "something to fight for." They had been told how the East Pakistanis burned Ali Jinnah's picture, along with the Pakistan flag, and how the Awami League intended to destroy the nation.

The slaughter went on for two days. It then settled into a relentless hunt and extermination of teachers and intellectuals whom the army blamed for the attempt to split the nation. Strangely enough, Mujibur Rahman, the only Awami leader who refused to flee, was not arrested until two days after the attack on Iqbal Hall. When military police finally drove up to his home, he told them that it was not necessary for them to have come for him. "Had you called me, I would have come," he said. Rahman was rushed out of East Pakistan and secretly imprisoned in West Pakistan.

During the initial attack in East Pakistan, Yahya Khan made a radio speech in West Pakistan. He lashed out at Mujibur Rahman's "acts of treason." Furiously, the Pakistani president stated:

The man [Mujibur] and his party are enemies of Pakistan and want East Pakistan to break completely from the country. He has attacked the solidarity and integrity of this country—

the crime will not go unpunished. We will not allow some power-hungry people to destroy this country . . . Sheikh Mujibur Rahman and his party have defied lawful authority. They have insulted Pakistan's flag and defiled the photograph of the Father of the Nation. . . . They have created terror, turmoil, and insecurity. Millions of our Bengali brethren and those who settled in East Pakistan are living in a state of panic. . . .

I should have taken action against Sheikh Mujibur Rahman and his collaborators weeks ago, but I tried my utmost to handle the situation in such a manner as not to jeopardize my plan of peaceful transfer of power. . . . I explored every possible avenue for arriving at some reasonable solution.

General Tikka Khan, Administrator of Military Law in East Pakistan, declared: "Let me make it absolutely clear that no matter what happens, as long as I am in command of the Pakistan Armed Forces and Head of State I will insure complete and absolute integrity of Pakistan. . . ." With Dacca under control, Tikka Khan sent his troops fanning out across East Pakistan to uproot centers of revolt. The East Pakistanis, refusing to be cowed, fought back, organizing a guerrilla group called the Mukti Bahini. The rebels declared independence and announced the formation of a Bangladesh government in exile.

As the extermination campaign of Tikka Khan continued, hundreds of thousands of Hindus and Bengalis fled across the border into India. Calcutta, the Indian city on the Hoogly River, became one vast refugee camp. The political situation was also overflowing beyond the borders of the two Pakistans. India had a paramount interest in the destruction of Pakistan. Therefore, it was actively aiding the Mukti Bahini and the Bangladesh government-in-exile. The United States and China, still political enemies at that time, found themselves on the same side, supporting Pakistan. Russia sided with India in supporting Bangladesh.

China's support of Pakistan was rooted in an armed clash between India and China in 1962. The trouble was over a border dispute. Suddenly fearful of China for the first time, India began to modernize her army and air force. Russia, the United States and Great Britain pledged aid to India. The United States was supplying military aid to Pakistan at the same time, but cut off assistance to both India and Pakistan after the Indo-Pakistan War of 1965. Russia quickly moved into the vacuum left by America's refusal to supply more arms, and provided India with tanks, artillery, and Sukhoi-7 fighter-bomber aircraft.

Both China and the United States were alarmed by this extension of Russian influence. Now, with Russian backing, India prepared for armed intervention in East Pakistan. According to Retired Major General D.K. Palit of the Indian Army, India did not intervene immediately after the March 25 attack because the rainy season was approaching. Then all East Pakistan would be inundated and military maneuvers impossible. India expected foreign intervention if she went to Bangladesh's aid and wanted to strike hard enough to win the war in a matter of days. This required a delay until fall or winter. A winter war had another advantage as well. Snow would close the mountain passes between China and India, lessening the chance of Chinese intervention. There was also a need to build up the Mukti Bahini guerrilla forces in East Pakistan.

In Bangladesh (formerly East Pakistan), the reign of terror continued. By the middle of April, more than one million refugees had fled into India. This increased to perhaps ten or twelve million before it stopped.

The Mukti Bahini stepped up their activities as they received Indian arms and support. This aid greatly increased after a West Pakistani delegation went to Peking and failed to get the all-out support it sought. Mrs. Indira Gandhi, the Indian premier, then decided that China would not risk an outright invasion of India because she was too involved in negotiations to ease the tension then existing with the United States. Chou En-lai, the Chinese premier, was negotiating with Dr. Henry Kissinger, special representative of President Nixon, for the American president to make his historic visit to China. Plans for this visit were announced in Peking in July, 1971. China's admission to the United Nations was also pending, and China did not want world opinion to turn against her at this crucial time.

Atrocities mounted in the self-proclaimed state of Bangladesh. David Loshak, the British journalist, described the terror as follows:

> Soldiers brainwashed on a course of Bengali race hatred were given their head. Whole villages were burned, hundreds of ordinary peasants shot or killed in more gruesome ways, even children bayoneted before their mothers' eyes and then left to die lingering deaths, girls raped and abducted. The martial-law leaders of Pakistan fully understood what they were doing.

Reports claimed that 300,000 Bengalis had been slaughtered. At first Tikka Khan had attempted to keep all journalists out of Bangladesh. When it proved impossible to cover up what the embattled Bengalis were calling "genocide," Tikka Khan claimed that any atrocities committed by his soldiers amounted to retaliation for worse actions by the Bengalis.

Despite denials by those espousing the Bangladesh cause, there were indeed many atrocities committed by the Bengalis. Loshak, certainly no West Pakistan sympathizer, was one of the few journalists to show both sides of the atrocity charges. His report on Pakistani army excesses has already been quoted in part. Here is what he has to say about the other side:

> As to the charges of Bengali atrocities—the gangster element in the Awami League and outside it had run amok. . . . While in the public parts of Dacca, Bengalis merely destroyed English language signs and non-Bengali signs, in more secluded places they attacked Punjabis and even Biharis—refugees from India who came after Partition. They hacked them to death, burnt them alive, cut their throats—men, women and children unsparingly.

The situation became so bad that Yahya Khan was forced to remove Tikka Khan as Martial-Law Administrator. Tikka remained a member of the military junta ruling Pakistan, but was reassigned as commander of a corps in West Pakistan. Another member of the ruling group, Lieutenant General A.A.K. Niazi, was sent to replace Tikka.

The Bangladesh guerrillas, with full Indian aid, were using the Indian border as a sanctuary from which they launched hit-and-run attacks against the Pakistani Army. Niazi—supposedly with the consent of Yahya Khan—threatened to pursue the rebels into India. At the same time, India became increasingly provocative and threatening toward Pakistan. Indian divisions were placed for a three-prong attack on Pakistan. War was considered inevitable in both Delhi (capital of India), and Islamabad (capital of Pakistan). However, the big powers did not seem to take this warning seriously.

Pakistan was encouraged by a $211 million loan from China and by resumed United States military aid. America's enemies claimed that Pakistan had played an important go-between role in arranging the initial Kissinger-Chou En-lai meeting and the United States Government therefore felt beholden to Yahya's regime.

The war that had been simmering all through the rainy summer and stormy fall broke out suddenly on December 3, 1971. There have been charges and countercharges over who provoked the actual shooting. The Indians claimed that the Pakistanis started it on the western front—that is, on the West Pakistan-Indian border. The Pakistanis charged that Indian armored columns began the war with a surprise thrust toward Dacca.

Although there was considerable fighting on the western front, it was actually only a diversion by the Indian Southern Command to bottle up Pakistani troops that might otherwise have been dispatched to Bangladesh. The defending Pakistani commanders in Bangladesh made a basic mistake when they assumed that the marshy land, cut as it is by thousands of streams, would bog down the invaders. Instead, the Indian Army thrust forward with a speed that bewildered the defenders—an exceptional example

The marshy land of East Pakistan, cut by a thousand streams was ill-fitted for fighting a war.

of military planning. Roads are so few and poor in Bangladesh that almost all transportation is by river. Accordingly, the troops went into battle carrying pontoon bridges to ford rivers; where this was impractical, fleets of helicopters converged to ferry soldiers across unmarchable land, marshes, and streams. When roads became too bad for trucks, ammunition and guns were reloaded on rickshaws that were pulled across the soft ground.

Since the war meant a confrontation between Russia, China, and the United States, none of the big powers were eager to see the struggle continue at this time. But Russia attempted to make political capital of the situation. Therefore, when the United States brought the matter before the Security Council of the United Nations, Russia vetoed the resolution which called for a cease-fire.

On December 6th, three days after the invasion of Bangladesh by Indian troops, Mrs. Gandhi announced that India officially recognized the Bangladesh Government-in-exile as the lawful government of the nation. In Washington, Columnist Jack Anderson, published secret documents of the National Security Council, showing U.S. favoritism toward Pakistan. The U.S. State Department issued the following statement: "We believe that since the beginning of the crisis, Indian policy in a systematic way has led to perpetuation of the crisis, a deepening of the crisis, and that India bears the major responsibility for the broader hostilities which have ensued."

President Nixon also ordered a task force from the U.S. Seventh Fleet, operating in Southeast Asian waters, to proceed to the Bay of Bengal. Jack Anderson claimed that the National Security Council papers showed that the nuclear-powered aircraft carrier "Enterprise" and supporting craft were sent to Indian waters to force India to divert planes and ships from the Pakistan and Bangladesh fronts and to weaken India's blockade of East Pakistan.

The United Nations General Assembly, irritated by the deadlock in the Security Council, passed a resolution on December 7, 1971 which demanded a ceasefire and an immediate withdrawal of troops by both sides. The vote was 104 to 11. Russia and its satellites joined India in voting against the resolution. France and Great Britain abstained, and the United States and China voted for the ceasefire. This ceasefire vote was a moral victory for Pakistan and a blow to India's pride, but it was not enforceable. Only the Security Council could authorize UN intervention and it was deadlocked by Russia's veto.

Indian forces thrust deeper into Bangladesh and then wheeled about to threaten Dacca. The Pakistani forces were crumbling. Large numbers began to surrender by December 11th, and by the 14th General Niazi sent an offer to surrender the entire Pakistani Army. The message was transmitted through the American Embassy in New Delhi. Indian troops moved into liberated Dacca on December 16th, and at 4:31 that afternoon Niazi signed the Instrument of Surrender. He presented it to Lieutenant General Jagjit Singh Aurora whose title was "General Officer Commanding in Chief Indian and Bangladesh Forces in the Eastern Theater."

Bangladesh was now officially a new nation, and East Pakistan had passed into history.

CHAPTER

14

Looking to
a Brighter Future

Yahya Khan's rule did not survive the military debacle in Bangladesh. Four days after the Instrument of Surrender was signed in Dacca, Yahya was forced to turn over the government to Zulfikar Ali Bhutto and his Pakistan People's Party. Yahya was placed under house arrest to remove him from politics and was still under arrest in 1974.

The new premier faced monumental problems. On the morning of December 16, 1971, his country was the fifth largest in the world, its population numbering 130 million. But at 4:21 p.m. that day, the figure dropped to 55,000,000. A quarter of the Pakistani Army was in prison camps in Bangladesh. The economy was ruined. At this point as much as 80 per cent of the country's foreign exchange had been earned by jute and rice exports from the now severed east wing of the country. The textile industry and cotton exports—the principle sources of foreign exchange for the west wing—had depended more on a captive market in Bangladesh than upon foreign sales. In addition to his social problems at home, Bhutto faced possible war with India. And on the Afghanistan front, the Pathans were agitating for an independent state to be called Pakhtoon. The dissidents were actively encouraged by the Afghan Government.

This desperate situation in Pakistan caused jubilation in Delhi, where Indian leaders were certain that collapse was just a matter of time. They also believed that Bangladesh would be unable to survive independently and that the two countries would then be reabsorbed into an India which would once again stretch from the Bay of Bengal to the Khyber Pass. But, instead of collapsing, Pakistan came out of the debacle stronger than ever.

Credit for this turn of events was entirely due to Zulfikar Ali Bhutto, who rewelded the shattered pieces of his nation's economic and political collapse. He was 43 years old when he wrested the premiership of Pakistan from Yahya Khan. Bhutto came from a wealthy family who owned large estates in the Indus Valley, and he is still said to be one of the largest landowners in the country. Since he heads a socialistic government dedicated to land reform, his own holdings are not a matter of public discussion. From the very first, he groomed himself for a political career. In 1950, he was graduated with honors in political science from the University of California, Berkeley. Then, in 1952, he took a master's degree with honors in law at Oxford, England. The following year he returned to Pakistan to practice law and teach constitutional law—and also to plunge head-first into politics.

Z.A. Bhutto first came on the international political scene in 1957, when Ayub Khan appointed him Pakistan's delegate to the United Nations General Assembly. However, he was not satisfied to be so far from the scene of national politics which had become his very life's blood. He managed to be recalled from New York in

1958, and at the age of thirty was named minister for commerce in Ayub Khan's cabinet. Within five years, he had moved through a succession of top cabinet positions to become foreign minister. But he was a leader, not a follower, and as soon as he saw an opportunity he struck out on his own.

There was great popular dissatisfaction over the Declaration of Tashkent which had ended the hostilities between India and Pakistan over Kashmir in 1966. At the time, Russia had arranged the Tashkent Conference. Now Bhutto resigned from the government and formed his opposition party—the Pakistan People's Party which has socialism as it basic plank. This socialistic program, plus his dramatic personal showmanship, won him a strong following.

In 1968, fearful of a general uprising, Ayub Khan had Bhutto arrested. But he was too popular to be kept in jail for long. When he was released, three months later, he began a strong electioneering campaign for the 1970 elections which were supposed to return Pakistan to civil government control. Bhutto's party swept the elections in West Pakistan, just as Mujibur Rahman's Awami League dominated the polls in East Pakistan.

When Ayub Khan was forced out, the new President Yahya Khan had to depend upon Bhutto and his strong following for support in the struggle to keep Mujibur Rahman from taking over the government. Bhutto then moved into total control when Yahya Khan's government collapsed, along with the Pakistan Army. Since Jinnah's death, all previous governments had been dominated—either openly or from behind the scenes—by the Pakistan Army high command. The collapse in Bangladesh and the imprisonment of a quarter of the troops as prisoners of war destroyed the army's prestige and allowed Bhutto's civilian government to dominate the military.

The country was in a desperate situation. Everyone realized as much, so there was little opposition when Bhutto initiated drastic reforms. Three days after he assumed power, he announced educational reforms to satisfy the restless students. Seventeen days after he became premier, Bhutto seized control of the country's ten basic industries in order to fit them into Pakistan's economic plan. However, ownership still remained with the so-called "twenty-two families" who supposedly controlled Pakistan's economy. In his campaign speeches, he had promised to nationalize all industry, but in the showdown he was forced to moderate his promises in order to prevent economic chaos. (Similarly, Mao Tse-tung had left some of China's major industries in the hands of their capitalistic former owners, when the Chinese Communist party took control in 1949.)

Bhutto next attacked the agriculture imbalance with a program called Integrated Rural Development. A government report described the program as follows:

> Under these reforms the ceilings of individual ownership was drastically cut . . . to 160 acres of irrigated or 300 acres of un-irrigated land. Land holdings in excess of the ceilings were taken without compensation and have been distributed among the peasantry free of cost. Government lands are now reserved for distribution among landless peasants.

Critics claim that the land reform program was only a token operation, and that it had little effect upon breaking up the large landowners' holdings.

Baluchistan, egged on by Afghanistan, caused trouble which ended in placing the province under martial law. In April, 1972, martial law was imposed upon the rest of the nation. Bhutto then became president under an interim Constitution, replaced by a new one in April, 1973. Under the new reorganization, which also provided for a national assembly of two houses, Bhutto became prime minister. The opposition members of the national assembly forced through amendments that made all laws subject to referral to a special Islamic council. When required, that body would decide if such laws were in conflict with Islam.

Bhutto's accomplishments on the diplomatic front were impressive. He succeeded in getting U.S. economic aid restored, but not military aid. He talked China into converting two of its largest loans into grants, and won an agreement with India to free the last Pakistani prisoners of war in Bangladesh. Mujibur Rahman had threatened to put 195 of them on trial as war criminals, but the agreement signed by Pakistan, Bangladesh, and India, in March, 1974, freed the prisoners without trial. Bhutto accomplished the prisoner release without making any major concessions.

The Wall Street Journal correspondent in Pakistan said the agreement made it appear almost as if Pakistan had won the war. The only minor concession Bhutto made was the inclusion of a single paragraph in the agreement which said that the Pakistan government "deplored and condemned" any crimes and atrocities that had been committed by the Pakistani Army during the war. He also agreed to withdraw opposition to the admission of Bangladesh into the United Nations. All new members must be approved by the United Nations Security Council, where China is one of the five nations holding veto rights. As a friendly gesture to Pakistan, China vetoed the admission of Bangladesh.

The prisoner of war agreement, engineered by Bhutto, was expected to greatly improve relations between India and Pakistan. But two months later—on May 18, 1974—India's scientists exploded a 10-kiloton nuclear device in an underground test in the Rajasthan Desert. The explosion was a stunning surprise to the entire world and an ominous forecast of future proliferation of nuclear weapons. Pakistan was particularly alarmed, having fought three wars with India in the past twenty-seven years.

Mrs. Indira Gandhi, assured the world: "We don't intend to use this knowledge or this power for any other than peaceful purposes. Our neighbors need have no fear." The prime minister's statement did not, however, reassure an uneasy world. India already had nuclear power plants, built with Canadian assistance. If her intentions were "peaceful," Bhutto said, "why was it necessary to build a bomb?"

Another very valid criticism of India's experiments with atom bombs concerns the desperate plight of her people. Millions are starving, food riots are wracking the country, and a bankrupt government is unable to do anything about its mammoth internal problems. Nevertheless, the country could spend the millions necessary to build an atom bomb.

Despite Pakistan's fear, the concensus among foreign diplomats was that development of the atom bomb by India was directed toward China who had sided with Pakistan in the Pakistan-Bangladesh war. This did not satisfy Bhutto. "Pakistan will eat leaves and grass, even go hungry," he said, "but we will have to get an atom bomb of our own."

This is possible because Pakistan also has a nuclear power plant, opened on November 28, 1972, at Karachi. It is of the same Canadian type that India used to convert from peaceful power production to the development of an explosive bomb. With this technology at his command, plus the recent discovery of rich deposits of uranium in Pakistan, Bhutto is in a position to make good his threat to develop his own nuclear weapons.

Apart from the threat of future nuclear war, Pakistan has other problems. One is the lack of personal freedom, although the situation is better now than at any other time since Pakistan became a nation. Still, Bhutto's domestic critics call him a "dictator." They point to arrests of opposition leaders (particularly in rebellious Baluchistan), muzzling of critical newspapers, strong-arm tactics by paramilitary elements of the prime minister's Pakistan People's Party, and Bhutto's wheeler-dealer approach to politics in general. Dictator or not, he seems to be ruling with the support of a large majority of his countrymen.

Apparently, the basic economy of Pakistan is adjusting to the separation from Bangladesh better than the former East Pakistan is doing. This is to be credited to Bhutto's policies and leadership However, he can do little about the underlying problem of conflicting groups. Pakistan is not an integrated country or nationality. One cannot categorize a "Pakistani" as one can a Frenchman or an Englishman. Pakistan is a federation of individual groups,

Men of Sind province: A nut seller in a village between Karachi and Thatta, and his friend.

Widespread illiteracy hampers the development of democracy in Pakistan. Here two professional letter writers ply their trade in Rawalpindi. The writer at right is reading a letter for an anxious man, worried about his mother's health. At left a writer awaits someone who wants a business letter typed.

each with its own culture and aspirations. The desert dwellers of Sind have little in common with the nomadic herdsmen of Baluchistan. The agriculturally rich Punjab is also different from the others. Like ill-fated East and West Pakistan, the religion of Islam is all they have to hold them together, and that has proven to be a fragile tie indeed.

Prodded by Afghanistan, the present insurgency in Baluchistan and the Northwest Territory can be expected to grow. Whether or not this will develop into another civil war, like the one that split Pakistan and Bangladesh in 1971, is uncertain. But the problem can be expected to continue to cause trouble and keep the nation divided.

The lack of civil liberties is not expected to change much. Those who deplore dictatorial governments fail to realize that democracy has a tough time surviving, even in countries where there is an enlightened electorate. In underdeveloped countries, where illiteracy is widespread, true democracy is impossible. The voters are at the mercy of any and all pressure groups and self-seeking political figures and parties. In such countries, the overthrow of one dictator only provides for the establishment of another, as the unhappy situation in South America continually proves.

In the immediate future, the best that Pakistan can hope for is a strong man who has the best interest of the country at heart. They seem to have one in Zulfikar Ali Bhutto.

APPENDIX

Important Dates
in Pakistan History

B.C.

30,000,000	Rising of the Himalaya Mounts creates Indus River
3,000	Probably beginning of Mohenjo-Daro civilization
2,300	Golden Age of Mohenjo-Daro
1,500	Invasion of Aryans and destruction of Mohenjo-Daro
327	Alexander the Great invades the Punjab
305	Chandragupta defeats Seleukos, preventing Greeks from reestablishing Alexander's Empire in India
200	Greeks reinvade the Punjab
180	Menander establishes Gandhara state in the Punjab
130	Sakas from Parthia destroys Indo-Greek state in Punjab

A.D.

47	Apostle Thomas introduces Christianity in Taxila
637	Mohammed and Islam triumph in Arabia
710	Arabs invade Sind and first introduce Islam in Pakistan
1398	Invasion by Tamerlane, the Earthshaker
1519	Babur the Tiger establishes Mogul Empire in India

1582   Akbar introduces his universal religion, *Din Ilahi*
1599   Queen Elizabeth I of England gives charter to East India Company
1650   British establish Fort William in Bengal
1757   Battle of Plassey begins East India Company's conquest of India
1842   Sir Charles Napier conquers Sind to begin conquest of what is now Pakistan
1845   First Sikh-Anglo War
1849   Punjab annexed by British to complete conquest of Indian subcontinent
1875 or 1876   Muhammed Ali Jinnah born in Karachi
1906   Moslem League formed
1926   Vicious Hindu and Moslem riots foreshadow future trouble
1935   Jinnah elected president of the Moslem League
1940   Jinnah calls for separate Moslem nation in India
1947   British leave India. Pakistan created on August 17th
1948   Jinnah dies; succeeded by Liaquat Ali Khan; fighting between Pakistan volunteers and Indian Army over Kashmir
1955   Ayub Khan becomes military dictator to avoid governmental collapse
1965   Indo-Pakistan War
1969   Mujibur Rahman issues his famous "six points" in his demand for East Pakistan autonomy
1971   Civil war between East and West Pakistan; new nation of Bangladesh formed from East Pakistan
1972   Bhutto displaces Yahya Khan as dictator; begins socialistic program
1974   Pakistan, Bangladesh, and India agree on settlement of long-standing prisoner-of-war controversy, opening way for resumption of diplomatic relations between Pakistan and Bangladesh

BIBLIOGRAPHY

Featherstone, Donald. *At Them With the Bayonets*. London: Jarrods, 1968.

Loshak, David. *Pakistan Crisis*. New York: McGraw-Hill, 1971.

Mahajan, Jagmahan. *Circumstances Leading to the Annexation of the Punjab*. Karachi: Kitabistan, 1949.

Majumdar, S. K. *Jinnah and Gandhi*. Calcutta: Firma Mukhopadhyay, 1966.

McCrindle, John W. *Ancient India as Described in Classical Literature*. Westminster (England): Archibald Constable, 1901.

McDonough, Sheila (ed.). *Mohammed Ali Jinnah*. Lexington (Massachusetts): D. C. Heath, 1970.

Moraes, Dom. *The Tempest Within*. Delhi: Vikas Publications, 1971.

Mosley, Leonard. *Last Days of the British Raj*. London: Widenfield & Nicholson, 1961.

Palit, Major General D. K. *The Lightning Campaign*. Salisbury (England): Compton Press, 1972.

Rawlinson, H. G. *India*. New York: Frederick A. Praeger, 1952.

Smith, Vincent A. *Early History of India*. London: Oxford University Press, 1924.

Srivasta, Ashirbadi L. *The Mogul Empire*. Agra (India): Shiva Lal Agarwala, 1957.

INDEX

Sukkar, 2, 4
Sulaiman Mountains, 38, 50, 78
Sutlej River, 2, 77, 85, 88–90
Suttee, 60
Syria, 41

Taj Mahal, 4, 63, 65
Tajuddin Ahmed, 140
Talpurs, Mirs, 73–74, 79–81
Tamerlane the Earthshaker, 4, 31, 46, 48, 51, 52, 163
Tashkent Treaty, 126–27, 134, 157
Taxes, 65, 130
Taxila, 8, 21, 23, 46, 48
  trade capital of North Pakistan, 30–33
  Apostle Thomas introduces Christianity in, 36–37, 163
  vassal state, 43
Teg Bahadur, 68
Tej Singh, 85, 88, 90–93
Thailand, 122
Thar Desert, 2, 7, 124–25
Thomas, Saint, 36–37, 163
Tibet, 1, 2, 34
Tikka Khan, General, 141, 148, 150–51
Timur; *See* Tamerlane the Earthshaker
Trade, 10, 36, 130
  routes, 20, 30, 47, 67
  in Taxila, 30–31
  in Sind, 79–80
Tuker, General Sir Francis, 106, 110, 147
Turkestan, 20, 51, 52
Turkey, 101, 122
Turks, invasion by, 43–46

U Thant, 126, 144
U-2 affair, 121–22

United Nations, 156
  discussion of Kashmir situation, 113, 114, 116
  China in, 123, 126, 149, 153, 159
  discussion of India-Pakistan war, 126, 152, 153
  aid to cyclone victims, 138, 144
  admission of Bangladesh, 159
United States, 130, 140
  aid to Pakistan, 120–26, 149, 151, 158–59
  aid to India, 124, 149
  aid to cyclone victims, 138
  relations with China, 149–50
  supported Pakistan in civil war, 152–54
Untouchables, 28
Ur of the Chaldees, 10, 23–24
Urdu language, 5, 8–9, 48

Vaisya, 28
Vale of Kashmir, 113, 114
Ventura, Jean Baptiste, 76
Vindapharna, 37
Vishnu, 25, 27
Visvanath, Temple of, 65

Water table, 16
Wavell, Lord, 106
Wellington, Duke of, 81, 87, 89, 91, 96
West Pakistan, 151
  established by partition, 4–5, 110, 112, 117, 119
  growing unrest, 128–29
  "Six Points", 130
  hatred for East Pakistan, 132, 138
  elections, 132–34, 136, 139, 157
  East Pakistan's independence movement, 140–42

About the Author

I. G. Edmonds was born in Texas and spent twenty-one years with the U.S. Air Force, serving much of the time in overseas locations in two wars. Since leaving the service in 1963, Mr. Edmonds has roamed the world on journalistic pursuits. He has written over seventy books, most of which are for young people. Mr. Edmonds presently lives with his wife and daughter in Cypress, California.